EYEWITNESS BOOKS

SUPER BOWL

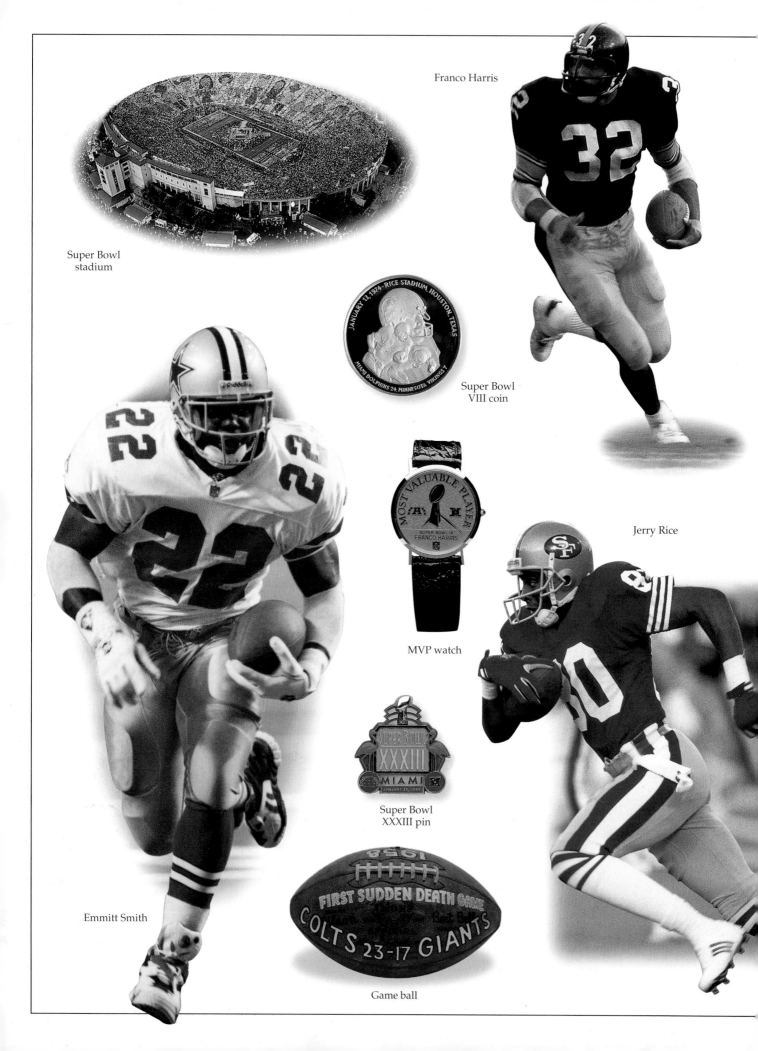

Super Bowl
stadium

Franco Harris

Super Bowl
VIII coin

MVP watch

Jerry Rice

Super Bowl
XXXIII pin

Emmitt Smith

Game ball

DK EYEWITNESS BOOKS

SUPER BOWL

Created by
NFL PUBLISHING
Written by
JAMES BUCKLEY JR.

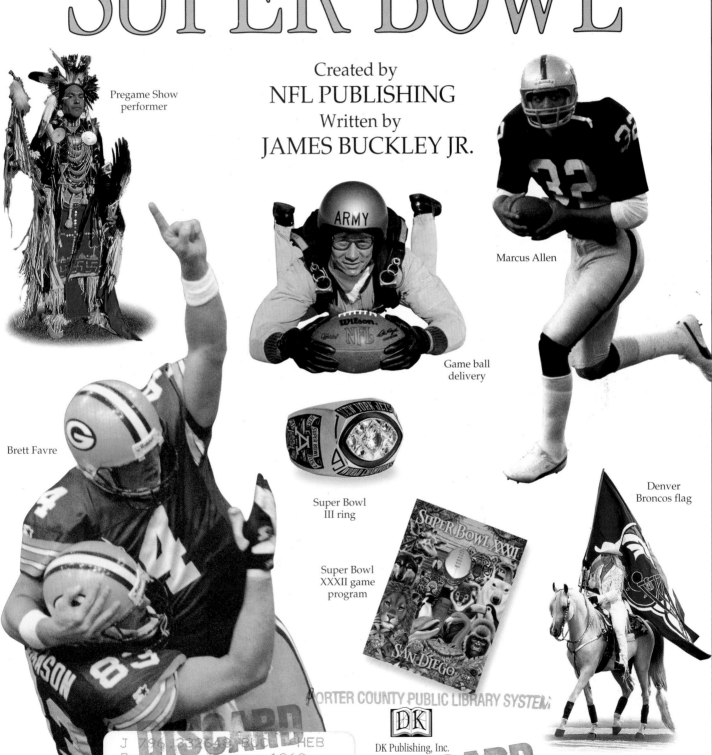

Pregame Show
performer

Game ball
delivery

Marcus Allen

Brett Favre

Super Bowl
III ring

Super Bowl
XXXII game
program

Denver
Broncos flag

DK

DK Publishing, Inc.

Super Bowl
XXX pin

Super Bowl
XXXI pennant

DK

LONDON, NEW YORK, MELBOURNE,
MUNICH, AND DELHI

Publisher Neal Porter
Executive Editor Iris Rosoff
Art Director Dirk Kaufman

Revised Edition
Project Editor Elizabeth Hester
Senior Art Editor Michelle Baxter
Publisher Chuck Lang
Creative Director Tina Vaughan
Production Chris Avgherinos

NFL CREATIVE
Editor-in-Chief John Wiebusch
Managing Editor John Fawaz
Project Art Director Bill Madrid
Director–Manufacturing Dick Falk
Director–Print Services Tina Dahl
Manager–Computer Graphics Sandy Gordon

Joe Montana

Terry Bradshaw

Second American Edition, 2003
2 4 6 8 10 9 7 5 3 1

Published in the United States by DK Publishing, Inc.
375 Hudson Street, New York, New York 10014
Copyright © 2003 NFL Properties LLC and DK Publishing, Inc.

DK Publishing books are available at special discounts for bulk purchases
for sales promotions or premiums. Special editions, including personalized
covers, excerpts of existing guides, and corporate imprints can be created in
large quantities for specific needs. For more information, contact Special
Markets Dept./DK Publishing, Inc./375 Hudson Street/New York,
New York 10014/FAX: 800-600-9098.

The National Football League, the NFL Shield logo, "NFL," "NFC," "AFC," and
"Super Bowl" are trademarks of the National Football League. The NFL team
names, logos, helmets, and uniform designs are trademarks of the teams indicated.

ISBN 0-7894-8831-0 (hardcover)
ISBN 0-7894-8832-9 (library binding)

John Elway

Printed in China.

Discover more at
www.dk.com

Contents

Before the Super Bowl

THE NATIONAL FOOTBALL LEAGUE was founded in 1920. Actually, it first was known as the American Professional Football Association; it became the NFL in 1922. And, like any league, it had to have a champion. From 1920 to 1932, the champion usually was the team with the best record; most often, there were no playoff games. The Akron Pros won the title in 1920. Beginning in 1933, the NFL split into Eastern and Western Divisions. The division champions played the NFL Championship Game to determine the league's overall winner. That game was played each season through 1969, when the NFL merged with the American Football League. The Super Bowl, played each January or February at a neutral site, then became the NFL's official championship game.

EARLY CHAMPIONSHIP TROPHY
The Cleveland Bulldogs won this trophy as the 1924 NFL champions. The Bulldogs originally played in Canton, Ohio. In 1924, the two-time defending NFL-champion club was purchased and moved to Cleveland. It disbanded after 1927. Notice the more bulbous shape of the 1920s-era ball on which this trophy was modeled.

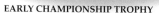
"Sudden death" in the NFL playoffs means that the first team to score in overtime wins the game.

FOOTBALL FROM A CLASSIC GAME
This painted ball honors the 1958 title game won by Baltimore. Many teams award these painted "game balls" to outstanding players or coaches.

THEN, EVERYTHING CHANGED
The NFL grew slowly throughout the 1950s. Baseball still was America's favorite sport, and college football boasted more fans than the pro game. But one particular NFL Championship Game, and the manner in which many people enjoyed it, changed American sports forever. In 1958, the Baltimore Colts, led by Johnny Unitas (19), defeated the New York Giants 23-17 in the first sudden-death overtime game in NFL history. The dramatic game was watched by millions on national television for the first time. The marriage between football and TV was an instant success. The game would prove to be the springboard to the Super Bowl's success in years to come.

Signature of Hall of Fame
defensive lineman Doug Atkins

DA BEARS
The Chicago Bears were one of the NFL's original teams, having started as the Decatur Staleys in 1920. In 1963, they won the last of their eight pre-Super Bowl NFL titles. This commemorative ball carries the signatures of the entire team.

COVERED IN GLORY
These program covers are from NFL Championship Games (1960, top, and 1949) won by the Philadelphia Eagles.

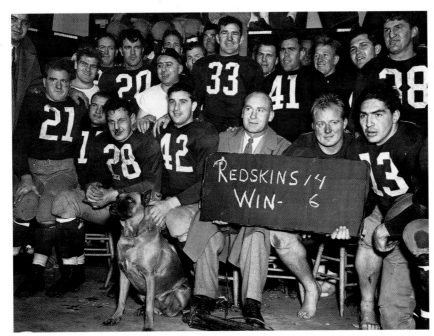

DURING THE WAR YEARS
The NFL continued to hold championship games during World War II. In 1942, the Washington Redskins (above) defeated Chicago 14-6, although the undefeated Bears were favored.

Early helmets were
made of leather.

Helmets were not
required until 1943.

Pads were sewn into
jersey and pants

FIRST GAME
In 1933, for the first time, the NFL planned an official championship game. The Chicago Bears (lateraling ball, right) defeated the New York Giants 23-21 at Wrigley Field in Chicago.

How the Super Bowl Was Born

I n 1960, THE AMERICAN FOOTBALL LEAGUE was created to challenge the NFL. Over the years, other leagues had come and gone in an attempt to match the NFL's success. The AFL came closest with eight teams (which eventually grew to 10 teams), and an exciting, wide-open style of play that caught fans' attention. Many AFL teams, notably the San Diego Chargers and Oakland Raiders, used exciting passing games. The AFL held its own championship game from 1960 to 1969, as well as its own college draft that lured some top players away from the NFL. Recognizing that cooperation would be better than competition, the NFL and AFL began to discuss a merger between the two leagues.

AFL logo

PART OF THE "FOOLISH CLUB"
Among the leaders of the new AFL were (left to right) Lamar Hunt of the Dallas Texans/Kansas City Chiefs (and also AFL founder), Ralph Wilson of the Buffalo Bills, Wayne Valley of the Oakland Raiders, and Billy Sullivan of the New England Patriots. They called themselves the Foolish Club.

THE MAN WHO MADE THE SUPER BOWL
In 1960, Los Angeles Rams executive Pete Rozelle was elected NFL commissioner. He would change sports in America like few other people. Rozelle led the negotiations with the AFL that created the Super Bowl. He also recognized the importance of television to the NFL's future.

TWO LEAGUES
The AFL used the logo at top left when the league was first formed. The NFL used the bottom logo for many years until modifying it slightly in 1981. After the merger, the AFL teams joined the NFL, which was split into the American and National Conferences. The Baltimore Colts, Cleveland Browns, and Pittsburgh Steelers moved to the new AFC to give each conference 13 teams.

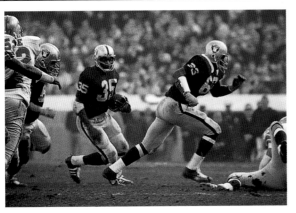

SEPARATE TITLES
The two leagues held separate title games throughout the 1960s. In 1967, the Oakland Raiders (left) won the AFL title game and later lost to Green Bay in Super Bowl II. The Packers (right) won five NFL titles in the decade: 1961-62 and 1965-67. The Packers have more NFL championships (12) than any other team.

Paul Hornung (5) set an NFL record by scoring 176 points in 1960.

PACKED HOUSE
This photograph of a sold-out Oakland Coliseum demonstrates the real challenge the AFL posed for the NFL. Fans were flocking to many of the AFL stadiums to enjoy top-quality, high-flying football action. The competition for players threatened the financial health of both leagues, leading to secret merger talks between NFL and AFL leaders that began in 1966.

ON THE WAY TO THE FIRST SUPER BOWL
Green Bay defeated Dallas in the 1966 NFL Championship Game and earned the right to represent the NFL in the first AFL-NFL Championship Game.

The Titans'—later the Jets—original colors were blue and gold.

THEY CALLED HIM BAMBI
One of the hallmarks of AFL football was spectacular passing plays. And no one made more of them than San Diego's Lance Alworth (19), shown here in the 1963 AFL Championship Game won by San Diego. Nicknamed Bambi for his graceful gait and bounding leaps, Alworth helped create today's modern downfield passing attacks. In 1978, he became the first AFL player elected to the Pro Football Hall of Fame.

TWO ORIGINALS
The Boston Patriots (helmet, above) were an original AFL team. In 1971, the team became the New England Patriots. In 1963, another original AFL team, the Titans (pennant, above), became the New York Jets.

Super Bowl I

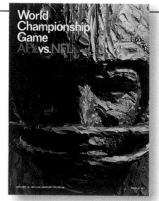

THE SUPER BOWL WAS BORN JUNE 8, 1966. Or, more accurately, on that day, NFL Commissioner Pete Rozelle announced the creation of the game that would become known as the Super Bowl. When the merger between the NFL and the AFL was announced, the two leagues agreed that their champions would meet in the postseason "AFL-NFL World Championship Game" to determine an overall champion. Following the 1966 season, the Kansas City Chiefs of the AFL and the Green Bay Packers of the NFL met on January 15, 1967. For the only time in Super Bowl history, the game was not a sellout. There were more than 30,000 empty seats in the Los Angeles Memorial Coliseum as 61,946 people witnessed a 35-10 victory by Green Bay...and the start of something really big.

WEIGHTY MATTERS
As with many things associated with the first Super Bowl, the game program has become a major collectible. The cover featured a close-up of a sculpture of a football player created by Jean Isaacson. The cover price was $1.

HE SHOWED THEM THE WAY
Green Bay coach Vince Lombardi was a star college player at Fordham, an assistant for the New York Giants in the 1950s, and the man who crafted one of football's greatest dynasties in Green Bay. Under Lombardi, the Packers won five NFL championships in seven seasons (1961-67).

SYMBOL OF VICTORY
The Packers were the first team to earn this most-coveted sign of NFL greatness: a Super Bowl ring. Green Bay's ring for Super Bowl I was made out of sterling silver and sported a single diamond in the crown.

Chiefs' coach Hank Stram had his players use this unique form of the huddle.

MARVELOUS MAX
Little-used receiver Max McGee was the unlikely star of Super Bowl I. Filling in for injured starter Boyd Dowler, McGee came off the bench to catch 2 touchdown passes from most valuable player Bart Starr (opposite, top left). In the third quarter, McGee made this juggling catch for a 13-yard touchdown.

ROCKET MAN!
In 1967, man had not yet landed on the moon, but space travel was all the rage. A unique bit of entertainment at Super Bowl I was the appearance of two men wearing rocket-propelled backpacks. They floated in over the rim of the stadium before settling down on the field before the game.

I GOT IT!
Although the Chiefs bottled up Green Bay receiver Carroll Dale on this play, they could not stop the powerful Packers' offense. Green Bay scored touchdowns in every quarter. It outgained Kansas City in total yards, 361 to 239.

KANSAS CITY, HERE THEY COME
The Chiefs were the first team to try to show that the upstart AFL was just as good as the long-established NFL. But they were not up to the task. Green Bay held Kansas City to only 1 touchdown and 1 field goal.

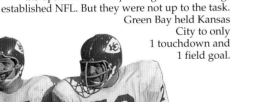

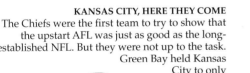

ALL PATCHED UP
This commemorative patch (made after the name "Super Bowl" first was officially used prior to the third AFL-NFL matchup) shows both the AFL and NFL logos.

HIT IT!
The pregame and halftime entertainment at the first Super Bowl pales in comparison to today's extravaganzas. New Orleans jazz trumpeter Al Hirt (right) played during the Pregame Show. The Halftime Show featured two college marching bands.

Super Bowls II, III, IV

Reporters covering Super Bowl II got a box lunch in this commemorative container.

GREEN BAY CONTINUED THE NFL'S DOMINANCE by defeating Oakland in Super Bowl II. The rival AFL teams had been thoroughly beaten in the first two Super Bowls. But in Super Bowl III, the unthinkable happened: The AFL defeated the mighty NFL. And the best part was that a brash young quarterback named Joe Namath had "guaranteed" the victory before the game. Namath's prediction—and the dramatic way he made it stand up—rocketed the Super Bowl onto the national sports map. The video image of Namath running off the field—waving his index finger to show who was number one—remains one of football's most memorable moments. With an NFL victory no longer a foregone conclusion, the Super Bowl quickly moved to the top of the sports scene, taking the first steps on the road to the dominant position it holds today.

SUPER BOWL II
Orange Bowl, Miami
GREEN BAY 33, OAKLAND 14

SUPER BOWL III
Orange Bowl, Miami
N.Y. JETS 16, BALTIMORE 7

SUPER BOWL IV
Tulane Stadium, New Orleans
KANSAS CITY 23, MINNESOTA 7

MAD BOMBER
Quarterback Daryle Lamonica of the Oakland Raiders led one of the most explosive offenses in football. But the Raiders couldn't solve the Packers' defense in Super Bowl II.

VITAL VICTORY
The Jets were 18-point underdogs to the mighty Baltimore Colts in Super Bowl III, but Joe Namath engineered a shocking 16-7 upset whose importance still resonates today. Namath was named the game's most valuable player.

Namath was as famous for his personality—and his trademark white football cleats—as for his talent.

A JOYFUL RIDE
Coach Vince Lombardi called riding on his players' shoulders "the best way to leave the field." After defeating Oakland in Super Bowl II, Lombardi enjoyed his final ride off the field. Soon after the game, he retired from coaching the Packers. He would go on to coach Washington for one season before dying of cancer in 1970.

SURPRISE HEROES
This pin heralds the Jets, who were the first AFL team to win the Super Bowl.

JOHNNY U
Not even future Pro Football Hall of Fame member Johnny Unitas (19) could save the Colts in Super Bowl III. The veteran Unitas came off the bench to lead the Colts to their only score.

Patch commemorating Super Bowl III

UNSCHEDULED LANDING
Before Super Bowl IV, pregame entertainment included a pair of hot-air balloons, one representing each team. However, the Vikings' balloon (right) foreshadowed Minnesota's fate in the game. The balloon crash-landed amid the spectators, draping its fading canopy over hundreds of people. There were no injuries, except perhaps the pilot's pride.

FROM NORWAY TO CANTON
Kansas City kicker Jan Stenerud, a native of Norway, kicked 3 field goals in the Chiefs' 23-7 victory over Minnesota in Super Bowl IV. Stenerud later became the first kicker elected to the Hall of Fame.

A PAIR OF STARS
Two veteran AFL players who had been part of Kansas City's Super Bowl I losing team enjoyed great days at Super Bowl IV. Receiver Otis Taylor (89) caught a 46-yard touchdown pass from Len Dawson, the game's MVP, while running back Mike Garrett (21) scored on a 5-yard run.

Kicking tee, used on kickoffs

THINGS CHANGE
Tickets for Super Bowl IV sold for $15. Some tickets to Super Bowl XXXIV, thirty years later, went for almost $400.

Super Bowls V, VI, VII

SUPER BOWL V AFTER THE 1970 SEASON was the first between the American Football Conference and the National Football Conference. Meanwhile, the popularity of the Super Bowl continued to grow. Although the first Super Bowl was not a sellout, every one that followed was a huge success. In only its fifth season, the game had become one of the most watched television programs of the year. In January, 1971, the Colts and Cowboys played the first game decided in the final seconds. Two years later, a Super Bowl victory gave one team the first perfect season in NFL history.

SUPER BOWL V
Orange Bowl, Miami
BALTIMORE 16, DALLAS 13

SUPER BOWL VI
Tulane Stadium, New Orleans
DALLAS 24, MIAMI 3

SUPER BOWL VII
Memorial Coliseum, Los Angeles
MIAMI 14, WASHINGTON 7

FIRST THE KICK, THEN THE LEAP
With this 32-yard field goal (above), Colts kicker Jim O'Brien (leaping, right) gave Baltimore a 16-13 victory over Dallas in Super Bowl V. The kick came with five seconds remaining in the game, the latest winning score in Super Bowl history. O'Brien, a rookie, was so nervous before the kick he tried to pull up blades of grass to check the wind. One problem: The game was played on artificial turf.

Square-toed kicking shoe

SO CLOSE, YET SO FAR
Dallas Cowboys cornerback Mel Renfro demonstrates the reaction of the losing team in Super Bowl V. The Cowboys fell just short of the Colts. But Dallas would wait only a year to change disappointment to joy.

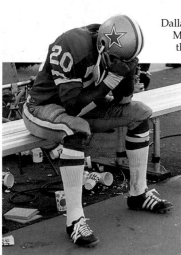

Patch made for Super Bowl VI showing host city

THEY WERE PERFECT
The Miami Dolphins completed the only perfect season (17-0) in NFL history with a 14-7 victory over Washington in Super Bowl VII. Safety Jake Scott (right) intercepted 2 passes and was named the game's most valuable player.

ZONK!
Bruising running back Larry Csonka of Miami played a big role in the Dolphins' march to perfection. In Super Bowl VII, he was the leading rusher, with 112 yards on 15 carries.

THE DODGER
Dallas quarterback Roger Staubach was the most valuable player of the Cowboys' Super Bowl VI victory. Staubach's terrific scrambling ability earned him the nickname "Roger the Dodger."

HE MADE UP FOR IT
Don Shula was the coach of the Colts' team that lost Super Bowl III. In 1972, he led the Dolphins to a perfect season. He later became the NFL's all-time winningest coach.

Commemorative medal struck for Dolphins' Super Bowl VII victory.

Players use eye black to lessen glare from the sun.

ON TOP OF THE WORLD
Coach Tom Landry of the Cowboys rides on the shoulders of his team after Dallas won Super Bowl VI. Landry led the Cowboys from 1960-1988, taking them to five Super Bowls and winning two.

A "KIICK" OUT OF IT
Running back Jim Kiick and the Dolphins lost to Dallas in Super Bowl VI, but had their revenge the next season, winning Super Bowl VII.

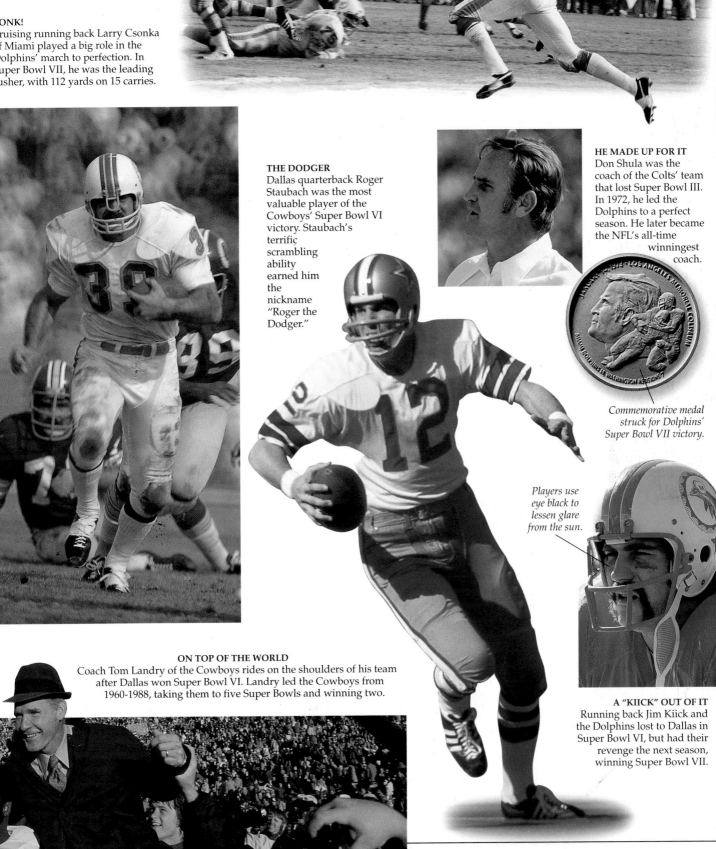

Super Bowls VIII, IX, X

Linebacker Bob Matheson's jersey number gave Miami's "53" defense its name.

AFTER ANOTHER VICTORY BY MIAMI, Pittsburgh made it four in a row for the AFC with wins in Super Bowls IX and X. The old NFL (or even NFC) dominance was truly finished, and the AFC was on the rise. From 1973-1981 (Super Bowls VII to XV), only Dallas would manage a victory in Super Bowl XII. But before that could happen, in 1976 America turned 200 years old and the Super Bowl turned 10. The game began to grow in popularity internationally, becoming one of the world's most popular single-day sporting events. The circus atmosphere and intense media attention were on an upward growth curve that continues today.

SUPER BOWL VIII
Rice Stadium, Houston
MIAMI 24, MINNESOTA 7

SUPER BOWL IX
Tulane Stadium, New Orleans
PITTSBURGH 16, MINNESOTA 6

SUPER BOWL X
Orange Bowl, Miami
PITTSBURGH 21, DALLAS 17

Super Bowl VIII medallion

MOST VALUABLE POUNDER
A year after its undefeated 1972 season, Miami returned to the Super Bowl to defend its NFL title. Running back Larry Csonka was the team's workhorse in Super Bowl VIII, running for a record 145 yards, including 5- and 2-yard touchdown runs. He was named the most valuable player of the Dolphins' convincing 24-7 victory over Minnesota.

Defensive backs cover opposing receivers—or try to (right).

DOLPHINS CAN FLY
The Dolphins lived on the ground for the most part in Super Bowl VIII. Quarterback Bob Griese attempted only 7 passes in the game, but he completed 6, including this one to Paul Warfield, a top receiver who would be elected to the Hall of Fame in 1983.

Harris won four Super Bowls with Pittsburgh.

HAPPY 200TH!
The Super Bowl X patch and program cover reflected the celebration of America's Bicentennial in 1976.

SUPER MOVIE
Before and during Super Bowl X, Hollywood met the NFL when scenes for the movie *Black Sunday* were filmed. In the movie, criminals try to disrupt the Super Bowl. Actor Robert Shaw (left) and director John Frankenheimer were on the sidelines before the game...and before filming started.

FRANCO!
After winning MVP honors in Super Bowl IX, Pittsburgh running back Franco Harris had another good day in Super Bowl X, helping the Steelers defeat Dallas 21-17.

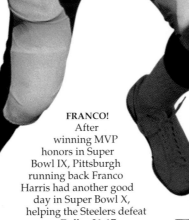

SUPER SWANN
Pittsburgh receiver Lynn Swann put on a show in Super Bowl X that still is regarded as one of the best days ever for a player in a Super Bowl. He had 4 spectacular catches for 161 yards and 1 touchdown. Swann, the game's MVP, made one catch (right) while falling sideways over a Dallas defender. His 64-yard touchdown catch proved to be the winning points.

THE STEEL CURTAIN
The key to the Pittsburgh Steelers' victory in Super Bowl IX was its powerful defense, nicknamed the "Steel Curtain," that held Minnesota to a record-low 17 rushing yards.

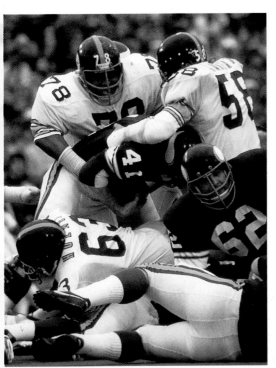

Super Bowls XI, XII, XIII

SUPER BOWL XI
Rose Bowl, Pasadena
OAKLAND 32, MINNESOTA 14

SUPER BOWL XII
Superdome, New Orleans
DALLAS 27, DENVER 10

SUPER BOWL XIII
Orange Bowl, Miami
PITTSBURGH 35, DALLAS 31

BY THE MID-1970S, THE SUPER BOWL had become bigger than ever. During the three games on these pages, records were set for attendance and television audience. More than 103,000 people filled Pasadena's Rose Bowl for Super Bowl XI, and more than 102 million fans watched Super Bowl XII. During this three-year span, a former AFL team (the Raiders) won the first of its three championships, Dallas's Doomsday Defense made its name, and Pittsburgh's AFC dynasty continued its dominance with the third of its four Super Bowl victories in six years.

Vikings' mascot from 1970s

MAN IN BLACK AND SILVER
Receiver Fred Biletnikoff combined grace, great hands, and the Oakland Raiders' legendary toughness. Biletnikoff was the most valuable player of Oakland's 32-14 victory in Super Bowl XI, the first of three NFL titles the former AFL franchise would earn.

FRAN THE MAN
When Fran Tarkenton retired in 1978, he was the NFL's all-time leader in attempts, completions, and touchdown passes. Unfortunately, he also was 0-3 in Super Bowls, including a loss in XI.

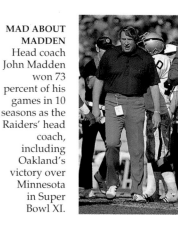

MAD ABOUT MADDEN
Head coach John Madden won 73 percent of his games in 10 seasons as the Raiders' head coach, including Oakland's victory over Minnesota in Super Bowl XI.

YES, THEY WERE
Gene Upshaw told the football world what the Raiders had become after Super Bowl XI. In 1987, Upshaw was elected to the Pro Football Hall of Fame.

Sign provided by fan after game.

Laces wrapped with athletic tape for tighter fit.

PARTY TOWN!

New Orleans, Louisiana, hosted four of the first dozen Super Bowls. Part of the city's appeal for fans coming to the games was its great tradition of jazz which enlivened everything from pregame parties to postgame parades.

SUPER MUG

Fans at Super Bowls filled their homes with souvenirs from the big game, such as this mug showing the two teams' helmets, the site, and date of the game.

SACKED!

Harvey Martin demonstrates what the Cowboys did to Denver and quarterback Craig Morton in Super Bowl XII. Co-most valuable player's Martin and Randy White led Dallas to a 27-10 victory.

Helmet with chinstrap

Wristband

GOLDEN ARM

Rifle-armed quarterback Terry Bradshaw led the Steelers to victory in Super Bowl XIII. Pittsburgh defeated Dallas 35-31 to become the first team to win three Super Bowls. Bradshaw completed 17 of 30 passes for 318 yards and 4 touchdowns, the last a Super Bowl record. He was named the most valuable player of the game.

TWO SUPER PAIRS OF HANDS

Pittsburgh receivers John Stallworth (left) and Lynn Swann were formidable weapons in Super Bowl XIII. Stallworth caught 2 touchdowns in the game, including a record 75-yard score. Swann caught an 18-yard touchdown pass.

EYES ON THE PRIZE

This fan shows just how outsized and outlandish Super Bowl souvenirs can be. Of course, Dallas fans could get a Cowboys' version of the same thing.

ORANGE TURNED YELLOW

Miami's Orange Bowl was the site of Super Bowl XIII. Workers used special equipment to paint one end zone yellow for Pittsburgh of the AFC.

AFC logo painted on one end zone. The NFC logo was on the other end zone.

Super Bowls XIV, XV, XVI

THE STEELERS MADE IT FOUR VICTORIES in six years in Super Bowl XIV. When Super Bowl XV rolled around a year later, the concerns of the "real" world made an impact on the game as never before. Fifty-two Americans had been held hostage in Iran for more than a year. The hostages were freed only days before the game in January, 1981. Their release added an extra sense of celebration to the Super Bowl. In Super Bowl XVI, San Francisco started a Super Bowl dynasty that would rival the Steelers for sustained excellence. Forty-Niners quarterback Joe Montana would become one of the Super Bowl's biggest stars.

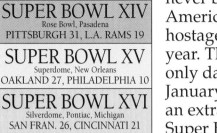

SUPER BOWL XIV
Rose Bowl, Pasadena
PITTSBURGH 31, L.A. RAMS 19

SUPER BOWL XV
Superdome, New Orleans
OAKLAND 27, PHILADELPHIA 10

SUPER BOWL XVI
Silverdome, Pontiac, Michigan
SAN FRAN. 26, CINCINNATI 21

A giant yellow ribbon on the Superdome welcomed home the hostages from Iran.

THE GO-AHEAD SCORE
John Stallworth (82) caught this 73-yard touchdown pass from MVP Terry Bradshaw to put the Steelers ahead for good in their Super Bowl XIV victory over the Los Angeles Rams.

THE TERRIBLE TOWEL
Before Super Bowl XIV, the symbol of Pittsburgh's faithful fans was unveiled in massive size. Steelers fans waved smaller versions of the yellow "Terrible Towels" to encourage their team to victory.

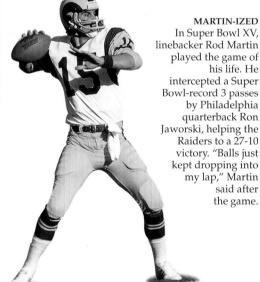

RAM TOUGH
Quarterback Vince Ferragamo led the Rams to their first Super Bowl appearance.

MARTIN-IZED
In Super Bowl XV, linebacker Rod Martin played the game of his life. He intercepted a Super Bowl-record 3 passes by Philadelphia quarterback Ron Jaworski, helping the Raiders to a 27-10 victory. "Balls just kept dropping into my lap," Martin said after the game.

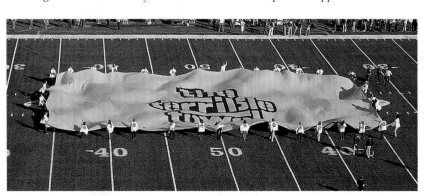

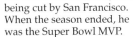

SURPRISE STAR
Raiders quarterback Jim Plunkett was a backup when the 1980 season started, two years removed from being cut by San Francisco. When the season ended, he was the Super Bowl MVP.

SPECIAL PIN
At each Super Bowl, members of the media receive special lapel pins used for identification; the pins also make a valuable souvenir.

TWO TDs
Speedy Cliff Branch was a favorite target of Plunkett's passes in Super Bowl XV. Branch made 5 catches in the game, including this one, a 29-yard touchdown in the third quarter. He also caught a 2-yard touchdown pass.

Bengals running back Charles Alexander stopped short of the goal line on third down by Dan Bunz (57).

SUPER JOE, PART I
San Francisco's Joe Montana accounted for 2 touchdowns, leading the 49ers' offense flawlessly and winning his first MVP award.

Goal line

THE MOTOR CITY
Super Bowl XVI was held in Pontiac, Michigan, on the outskirts of Detroit. The cover of the Super Bowl program featured depictions of automobile hood ornaments. Detroit is famous for its auto factories.

GOAL-LINE STAND
In a key series in the third quarter, the 49ers stopped the Bengals from reaching the end zone three times from the 1-yard line. It was the turning point in the 49ers' 26-21 victory.

FROZEN FOOTBALL
Super Bowl XVI was the first Super Bowl held in a northern city. There was no snow in the Silverdome, but outside it was cold enough for this ice sculpture.

Super Bowls XVII, XVIII, XIX

By THE MID-1980s, A PATTERN WAS EMERGING around the Super Bowl. Each year, the game got bigger and more popular, and each year, different story lines were written to draw even more attention to the game. The story lines for this trio of games were as follows:

Before Super Bowl XVII, the story was Washington's "Hogs" offensive line against Miami's "Killer Bees" defense (the Hogs won).

Before Super Bowl XVIII, fans and reporters wondered whether the Raiders' attacking defense could shut down the Redskins' record-setting offense (they could). And in Super Bowl XIX, would Super Bowl XVI hero Joe Montana be replaced by young, record-setting superstar Dan Marino of the Dolphins (no, he wouldn't)? And so the stories of the Super Bowl continued.

SUPER JOE, PART II
In Super Bowl XIX, Joe Montana continued his march toward Super Bowl greatness. He passed for 3 touchdowns and a record 331 yards, and he scored on a 6-yard run. He became only the third player to win two MVP awards, joining Bart Starr and Terry Bradshaw.

Washington's receivers called themselves "The Fun Bunch," and celebrated touchdowns with this leaping group high-five.

SUPER BOWL XVII
Rose Bowl, Pasadena
WASHINGTON 27, MIAMI 17

SUPER BOWL XVIII
Tampa Stadium, Tampa
L.A. RAIDERS 38, WASHINGTON 9

SUPER BOWL XIX
Stanford Stadium, Stanford, California
SAN FRANCISCO 38, MIAMI 16

As the designated "home" team, the 49ers wore their red home jerseys.

IN THE AIR AND ON THE GROUND
Running back Roger Craig was perfect for San Francisco's multifaceted attack. In Super Bowl XIX, he scored a record 3 touchdowns, including 2 on pass receptions and 1 on a 2-yard run.

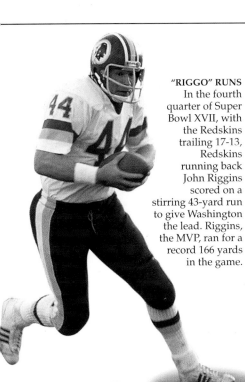

"RIGGO" RUNS
In the fourth quarter of Super Bowl XVII, with the Redskins trailing 17-13, Redskins running back John Riggins scored on a stirring 43-yard run to give Washington the lead. Riggins, the MVP, ran for a record 166 yards in the game.

TOUCHDOWN CATCH
Washington receiver Alvin Garrett caught this pass from Joe Theismann for a 4-yard touchdown. The Redskins won their first NFL championship since 1942.

Marino was renowned for his quick release on passes.

MARCUS WAS THE MAN
Super Bowl XVIII MVP Marcus Allen made one of the Super Bowl's greatest plays—a field-crossing, cutback, 74-yard touchdown run on the final play of the third quarter.

48 WAS NOT ENOUGH
In 1984, Dan Marino set NFL records with 48 touchdown passes and 5,084 yards. But the 49ers' defense shut down Marino in Super Bowl XIX.

SKY-HIGH GUY
Raiders punter Ray Guy made an important play early in Super Bowl XVIII, leaping to snag this high snap. He landed and got off a 42-yard punt, adding to his reputation as perhaps the greatest NFL punter ever.

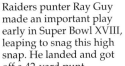

FISH MEETS "MAN"
Before Super Bowl XIX, the two opposing team mascots known as "Huddles" shook hands. Or at least fins.

SUPER VIEW
The tickets for Super Bowl XIX featured the Golden Gate Bridge, located in San Francisco, California.

Super Bowls XX, XXI, XXII

As the Super Bowl turned 20, it turned a new page in popularity, thanks to a song called "Super Bowl Shuffle." In 1985, the Chicago Bears had one of the most dominant teams in NFL history, with a powerful defense and a multifaceted offense. After 12 games they had recorded the song that would become their trademark. And, thanks mostly to a free-spirited style of play, they were enormously popular. They also had a player who would become an international superstar as much for his girth as his talent. William Perry, known from Chicago to London as "The Fridge," helped galvanize attention on the Super Bowl as few other players ever had. The game, already a national obsession, grew even bigger. Super Bowl XX became the most-watched television program in history, with more than 127 million people tuning in. *"We're not here to make no trouble/We're just here to do the Super Bowl Shuffle!"*

THE FRIDGE
There had been Super Bowl heroes before, from Namath to Montana. But there had never been a Super Bowl folk hero until William (The Refrigerator) Perry stomped into America's living rooms. Perry, a 300-pound defensive tackle, scored on a 1-yard run in Super Bowl XX, making him one of football's unlikeliest heroes.

Fans of "Da Bears"

SWEETNESS
Running back Walter Payton (34) of the Chicago Bears was nicknamed "Sweetness" for his silky (yet solid) style as well as his personal grace. In Super Bowl XX, he helped the Bears to a 46-10 victory over New England. Payton retired in 1987 as the NFL's all-time leading runner. His tragic death from cancer in 1999 saddened the sports world.

TOP OF THE WORLD
In Super Bowl XXI, another long-time NFL franchise returned to the top of the league. The New York Giants, founded in 1925, defeated Denver 39-20. Here, Mark Bavaro lifts Phil McConkey after the latter caught a touchdown pass that had bounced off Bavaro.

BACK ON TOP AGAIN
Die-hard fans of the Chicago Bears loyally stuck by their team through some very lean years in the late 1960s and 1970s. The Bears were one of the NFL's original franchises, founded in 1920. They had not won an NFL title since 1963.

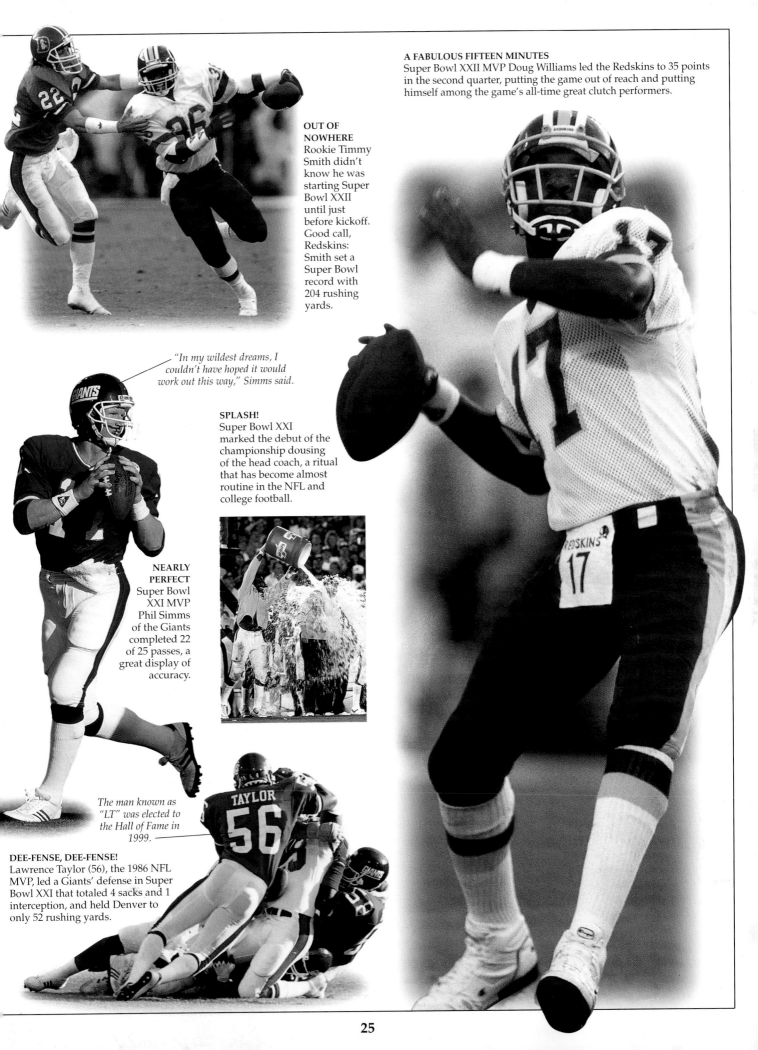

A FABULOUS FIFTEEN MINUTES
Super Bowl XXII MVP Doug Williams led the Redskins to 35 points in the second quarter, putting the game out of reach and putting himself among the game's all-time great clutch performers.

OUT OF NOWHERE
Rookie Timmy Smith didn't know he was starting Super Bowl XXII until just before kickoff. Good call, Redskins: Smith set a Super Bowl record with 204 rushing yards.

"In my wildest dreams, I couldn't have hoped it would work out this way," Simms said.

SPLASH!
Super Bowl XXI marked the debut of the championship dousing of the head coach, a ritual that has become almost routine in the NFL and college football.

NEARLY PERFECT
Super Bowl XXI MVP Phil Simms of the Giants completed 22 of 25 passes, a great display of accuracy.

The man known as "LT" was elected to the Hall of Fame in 1999.

DEE-FENSE, DEE-FENSE!
Lawrence Taylor (56), the 1986 NFL MVP, led a Giants' defense in Super Bowl XXI that totaled 4 sacks and 1 interception, and held Denver to only 52 rushing yards.

Super Bowls XXIII, XXIV, XXV

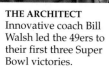

SUPER BOWL XXIII	Joe Robbie Stadium, Miami SAN FRAN. 20, CINCINNATI 16
SUPER BOWL XXIV	Superdome, New Orleans SAN FRANCISCO 55, DENVER 10
SUPER BOWL XXV	Tampa Stadium, Tampa N.Y. GIANTS 20, BUFFALO 19

THIS TRIO OF SUPER BOWLS HAD EVERYTHING. In successive years, fans enjoyed one of the greatest game-winning drives in NFL history in XXIII, the most dominating offensive performance in Super Bowl history in XXIV, and the combination of total joy and gut-wrenching agony that was Super Bowl XXV. The Super Bowl wrapped up its first quarter-century with games that featured superstars (Joe Montana and Jerry Rice) doing what they do best, and with a missed field goal that forever made the words "wide right" a meaningful part of the NFL vocabulary. Super Bowl XXV was decided when Buffalo's Scott Norwood missed a 47-yard field-goal attempt—wide right. But to Bills' fans credit, they greeted Norwood with a standing ovation at a city ceremony.

THE ARCHITECT
Innovative coach Bill Walsh led the 49ers to their first three Super Bowl victories.

DOMINATION
The 49ers' offense completely controlled Super Bowl XXIV, outgaining Denver in total yards (461 to 167) and setting a record with 55 points.

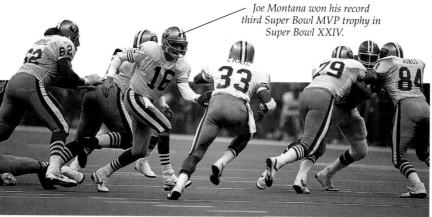

Joe Montana won his record third Super Bowl MVP trophy in Super Bowl XXIV.

Patch celebrating New Orleans, home to Super Bowl XXIV

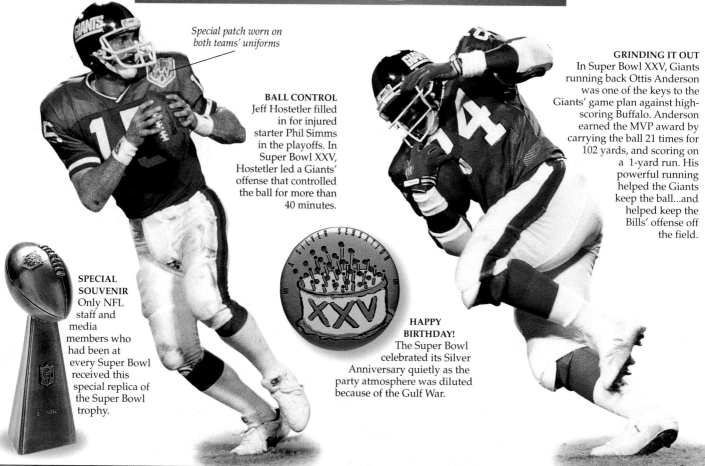

Special patch worn on both teams' uniforms

BALL CONTROL
Jeff Hostetler filled in for injured starter Phil Simms in the playoffs. In Super Bowl XXV, Hostetler led a Giants' offense that controlled the ball for more than 40 minutes.

GRINDING IT OUT
In Super Bowl XXV, Giants running back Ottis Anderson was one of the keys to the Giants' game plan against high-scoring Buffalo. Anderson earned the MVP award by carrying the ball 21 times for 102 yards, and scoring on a 1-yard run. His powerful running helped the Giants keep the ball...and helped keep the Bills' offense off the field.

SPECIAL SOUVENIR
Only NFL staff and media members who had been at every Super Bowl received this special replica of the Super Bowl trophy.

HAPPY BIRTHDAY!
The Super Bowl celebrated its Silver Anniversary quietly as the party atmosphere was diluted because of the Gulf War.

RICE WAS NICE
Receiver Jerry Rice was the Super Bowl XXIII MVP after catching 11 passes for a Super Bowl-record 215 yards. Rice's 8 career Super Bowl touchdowns also are the most ever.

Rice, like many receivers, wears special gloves that give him a better grip on the ball.

GAME WINNER
John Taylor (82) caught this 10-yard touchdown pass from Joe Montana with 34 seconds left in Super Bowl XXIII. Montana led the 49ers to this winning score after a 92-yard drive in less than three minutes.

WIDE RIGHT
Buffalo kicker Scott Norwood set off a Giants' celebration when he missed this 47-yard field-goal attempt with four seconds left that would have given Buffalo its first Super Bowl victory.

READY JUST IN CASE
Hats are made for both teams so the winners can wear them at the end of games. The Bills lost four Super Bowls and never got to wear this cap.

THE JOY OF VICTORY
Giants cornerback Everson Walls celebrates as Norwood's kick sails wide right. The Giants' exuberant postgame celebration reflected the intensity of the game that preceded it.

MAY WE SEE YOUR PASS?
Security always is tight at Super Bowls. This pass was worn by league officials at Super Bowl XXV.

SUPER BOWL XXV
Official

27

Super Bowls XXVI, XXVII, XXVIII

Minneapolis's Metrodome was home to Super Bowl XXVI, the northern-most game ever played.

THE SUPER BOWL HAS CREATED several dynasties; that is, teams that have returned repeatedly to the championship stage. The three games on this page represent three parts of one of the most unusual dynasties, that of the Buffalo Bills. From 1990 to 1993, the Bills were the AFC champions and became the only team to reach four consecutive Super Bowls. Unfortunately, they also were the only team to lose four consecutive Super Bowls. The Bills lost close Super Bowls (XXV) and blowout Super Bowls (XXVII). They played well (XXVIII) and not so well (XXVII again). They became the only team to lose Super Bowls to the same team in consecutive years (to Dallas in XXVII and XXVIII). However, their continued effort to return year after year in the face of disappointment remains a remarkable story of achievement.

SUPER BOWL XXVI
Metrodome, Minneapolis
WASHINGTON 37, BUFFALO 24

SUPER BOWL XXVII
Rose Bowl, Pasadena
DALLAS 52, BUFFALO 17

SUPER BOWL XXVIII
Georgia Dome, Atlanta
DALLAS 30, BUFFALO 13

RYPIEN RIPPED 'EM
Washington quarterback Mark Rypien entered Super Bowl XXVI as an unheralded passer. He left as the game's most valuable player, completing 18 of 33 passes for 292 yards and 2 touchdowns. It was the Redskins' third Super Bowl title in 10 years.

Quarterbacks sometimes wear small towels to wipe their hands between plays.

The Super Bowl XXVI pin featured a magical ice palace design for the Minneapolis game.

MARVELOUS MONK
Redskins receiver Art Monk (81) had 7 catches for 113 yards in Super Bowl XXVI. Monk retired in 1995 as the NFL's all-time leading receiver.

KING OF THE COWBOYS
Troy Aikman was the number-one overall pick in the 1989 NFL draft. Four years later, he proved that Dallas had chosen wisely by leading the Cowboys to victory in Super Bowl XXVII. Aikman passed for 4 touchdowns and was named the game's MVP.

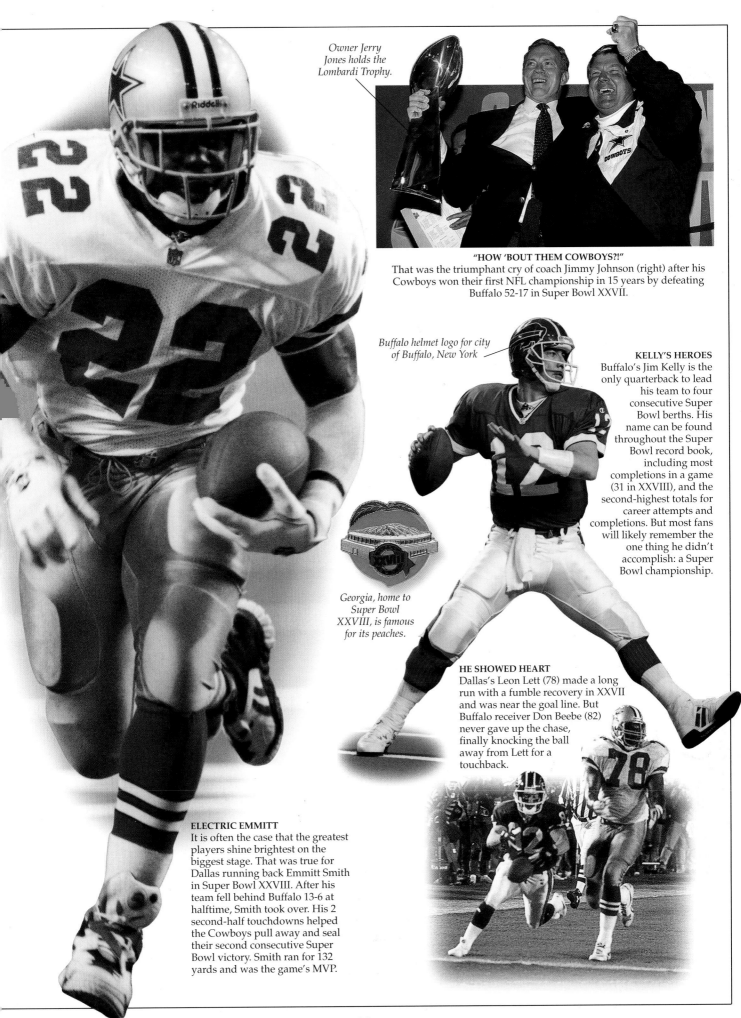

Owner Jerry Jones holds the Lombardi Trophy.

"HOW 'BOUT THEM COWBOYS?!"
That was the triumphant cry of coach Jimmy Johnson (right) after his Cowboys won their first NFL championship in 15 years by defeating Buffalo 52-17 in Super Bowl XXVII.

Buffalo helmet logo for city of Buffalo, New York

KELLY'S HEROES
Buffalo's Jim Kelly is the only quarterback to lead his team to four consecutive Super Bowl berths. His name can be found throughout the Super Bowl record book, including most completions in a game (31 in XXVIII), and the second-highest totals for career attempts and completions. But most fans will likely remember the one thing he didn't accomplish: a Super Bowl championship.

Georgia, home to Super Bowl XXVIII, is famous for its peaches.

HE SHOWED HEART
Dallas's Leon Lett (78) made a long run with a fumble recovery in XXVII and was near the goal line. But Buffalo receiver Don Beebe (82) never gave up the chase, finally knocking the ball away from Lett for a touchback.

ELECTRIC EMMITT
It is often the case that the greatest players shine brightest on the biggest stage. That was true for Dallas running back Emmitt Smith in Super Bowl XXVIII. After his team fell behind Buffalo 13-6 at halftime, Smith took over. His 2 second-half touchdowns helped the Cowboys pull away and seal their second consecutive Super Bowl victory. Smith ran for 132 yards and was the game's MVP.

Super Bowls XXIX, XXX, XXXI

SUPER BOWL XXIX
Joe Robbie Stadium, Miami
SAN FRANCISCO 49, SAN DIEGO 26

SUPER BOWL XXX
Sun Devil Stadium, Tempe, Arizona
DALLAS 27, PITTSBURGH 17

SUPER BOWL XXXI
Superdome, New Orleans
GREEN BAY 35, NEW ENGLAND 21

THE NATIONAL FOOTBALL LEAGUE celebrated its 75th anniversary during the 1994 season. The league named its All-Time Team, and players wore special patches on their uniforms all season. At Super Bowl XXIX after that season, many events were held to mark the occasion. During the game, one of the members of the All-Time Team put a final sparkling candle on the league's birthday cake. Jerry Rice, one of four receivers on the anniversary team, caught a 44-yard touchdown pass on the game's third play. The celebration continued in the next two Super Bowls, as former champions returned to the top.

75TH-ANNIVERSARY BANNER
This banner was displayed at Super Bowl XXIX.

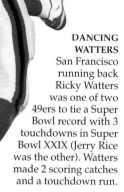

Numerals on NFL jerseys are about 11 inches high.

DANCING WATTERS
San Francisco running back Ricky Watters was one of two 49ers to tie a Super Bowl record with 3 touchdowns in Super Bowl XXIX (Jerry Rice was the other). Watters made 2 scoring catches and a touchdown run.

STEVE'S SILVER
San Francisco quarterback Steve Young put on a super show in Super Bowl XXIX. The lefty passed for 325 yards and a record 6 touchdowns. Why is this man smiling? He holds the Lombardi Trophy and was the game's MVP.

THE MAN IN CHARGE
The unseen hero of every Super Bowl since XIV is Jim Steeg, the NFL's senior vice president of special events. He is in charge of making every Super Bowl a successful one.

LOCAL HERITAGE
Native American dancers were part of the Super Bowl XXX pregame show, honoring Arizona's original inhabitants.

Rarely seen players' pin from Super Bowl XXX

JAY'S WAY
Tight end Jay Novacek (84) was one of many Dallas heroes in the Cowboys' 27-17 victory over Pittsburgh in Super Bowl XXX. The Steelers' defense, including Greg Lloyd (95), gave Dallas a scare, but a late interception by the Cowboys iced the game.

UNLIKELY HERO
Dallas cornerback Larry Brown became the first defender since Chicago's Richard Dent in Super Bowl XX to earn MVP honors. Brown made 2 key interceptions for Dallas in XXX.

Receivers often wear leather and nylon gloves.

Players in XXXI wore this patch to honor former NFL Commissioner Pete Rozelle, who had died shortly before the game.

MANY HAPPY RETURNS
Desmond Howard's 99-yard kickoff return for a touchdown helped seal Green Bay's victory in Super Bowl XXXI. He became the first special-teams player named the game's MVP.

SUPER EFFORT
New England rookie receiver Terry Glenn (in white, above) made one of the best catches in Super Bowl history on this 44-yard pass play in Super Bowl XXXI.

NO. 1...AGAIN
The Green Bay Packers had won Super Bowls I and II...but no more until Brett Favre (4) led the Packers back to the top of the NFL. Favre had 2 long touchdown passes and a touchdown run to help his team defeat the Patriots 35-21 in Super Bowl XXXI.

Super Bowls XXXII, XXXIII, XXXIV

SUPER BOWL XXXII
Qualcomm Stadium, San Diego
DENVER 31, GREEN BAY 24

SUPER BOWL XXXIII
Pro Player Stadium, Miami
DENVER 34, ATLANTA 19

SUPER BOWL XXXIV
Georgia Dome, Atlanta
ST. LOUIS 23, TENNESSEE 16

THE 1900S EARNED THE NICKNAME, at least in the world of sports, as the "NFL Century." As that century drew to a close, the Denver Broncos, led by veteran quarterback John Elway and young running back Terrell Davis, won consecutive Super Bowl titles. It was redemption for Elway, who had led the Broncos to three previous Super Bowls, only to lose each time. For Davis, it capped a journey from sixth-round pick to 2,000-yard rusher and Super Bowl MVP. But Davis' journey was easy compared to Kurt Warner. Warner was an undrafted free agent whose route to NFL stardom included a stop as a grocery bagger and stints in the Arena League and NFL Europe. Warner led the St. Louis Rams went from 4-12 in 1998 to 13-3 in 1999 and Super Bowl XXXIV, where they faced another surprising team, the Tennessee Titans. The Rams and Titans produced the most fantastic finish in the Super Bowl's 34-year history.

The Broncos, back in the Super Bowl for the first time in eight years, sported a new look—featuring a new logo and different-colored uniform.

Denver's mascot was riding high after the team's Super Bowl wins.

QUITE A CAPPER
In his final NFL game, John Elway went out in style. Elway led the Broncos to their second consecutive Super Bowl championship, defeating Atlanta 34-19. He passed for 336 yards and 1 touchdown and was the game's MVP.

This special pin, complete with Florida's pink flamingos, was given only to players.

TDs FOR T.D.
Terrell Davis lived up to his initials while earning MVP honors in Super Bowl XXXII. Davis set a Super Bowl record with 3 rushing touchdowns, including the game-winner with less than two minutes remaining. His powerful running, for a total of 157 yards, was key to Denver's first NFL championship.

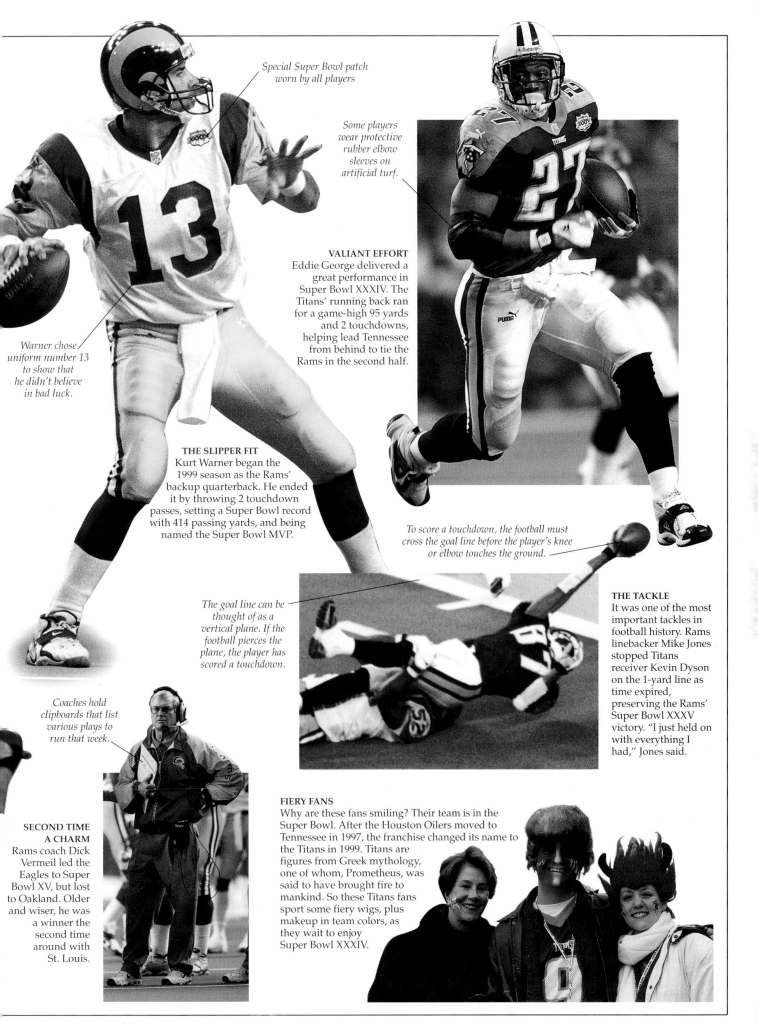

Special Super Bowl patch worn by all players

Some players wear protective rubber elbow sleeves on artificial turf.

VALIANT EFFORT
Eddie George delivered a great performance in Super Bowl XXXIV. The Titans' running back ran for a game-high 95 yards and 2 touchdowns, helping lead Tennessee from behind to tie the Rams in the second half.

Warner chose uniform number 13 to show that he didn't believe in bad luck.

THE SLIPPER FIT
Kurt Warner began the 1999 season as the Rams' backup quarterback. He ended it by throwing 2 touchdown passes, setting a Super Bowl record with 414 passing yards, and being named the Super Bowl MVP.

To score a touchdown, the football must cross the goal line before the player's knee or elbow touches the ground.

The goal line can be thought of as a vertical plane. If the football pierces the plane, the player has scored a touchdown.

THE TACKLE
It was one of the most important tackles in football history. Rams linebacker Mike Jones stopped Titans receiver Kevin Dyson on the 1-yard line as time expired, preserving the Rams' Super Bowl XXXV victory. "I just held on with everything I had," Jones said.

Coaches hold clipboards that list various plays to run that week.

SECOND TIME A CHARM
Rams coach Dick Vermeil led the Eagles to Super Bowl XV, but lost to Oakland. Older and wiser, he was a winner the second time around with St. Louis.

FIERY FANS
Why are these fans smiling? Their team is in the Super Bowl. After the Houston Oilers moved to Tennessee in 1997, the franchise changed its name to the Titans in 1999. Titans are figures from Greek mythology, one of whom, Prometheus, was said to have brought fire to mankind. So these Titans fans sport some fiery wigs, plus makeup in team colors, as they wait to enjoy Super Bowl XXXIV.

Super Bowls XXXV, XXXVI

DEFENSE WINS CHAMPIONSHIPS. The motto can be attributed to any sport, and though it may be cliché, it always seem to hold true. In Super Bowl XXXV, the Baltimore Ravens used a ferocious defense to allow just over 10 points per game—the fewest points allowed in the NFL since 1977—and a ball-control offense to suffocate opponents. The New York Giants were no match for the Ravens' defensive speed and tenacity. In four postseason games, the Ravens' defense allowed just one offensive touchdown. In Super Bowl XXXVI, the roles were reversed as the defensive team, the New England Patriots, was not expected to win. However, the Patriots forced 3 turnovers, which they turned into 17 points, to take a 17-3 lead. The high-scoring St. Louis Rams battled back to tie the game, but Adam Vinatieri's field goal as time expired once again proved the cliché correct.

HIGH-FLYER
A stealth bomber flew overhead during the National Anthem of Super Bowl XXXV.

HERE'S TO BALTIMORE
Ravens coach Brian Billick proudly hoists the Super Bowl XXXV Lombardi trophy. It was the first NFL title for the city of Baltimore since 1970.

Players wear gloves on their hands to get a better grip on their opponents.

EVERYBODY LOVES RAY
Baltimore linebacker Ray Lewis was the heart and soul of a Ravens defense that allowed the fewest points in the league since the NFL went to a 16-game schedule in 1978. The stifling defense did not allow an offensive touchdown in Super Bowl XXXV (the Giants' lone score was on a kickoff return), and Lewis earned most valuable player honors.

MARSHALL LAW
The Patriots' defense stymied Rams running back Marshall Faulk (left), limiting him to just 76 rushing yards and 54 receiving yards.

HAPPY LANDING
Patriots wide receiver David Patten made this twisting, leaping 8-yard touchdown catch with just 31 seconds left in the first half to give New England a 14-3 halftime lead. The touchdown came five plays after a Rams turnover.

ONE FOR THE AGES
Super Bowl XXXVI marked the first time the game ended on the final play. Patriots kicker Adam Vinatieri (4) drilled a 48-yard field goal (left) and then jubilantly celebrated (right, with holder Ken Walter) as time expired for New England's first Super Bowl title.

TOM TERRIFIC
Patriots quarterback Tom Brady earned Super Bowl XXXVI MVP honors, thanks to his game-winning 53-yard drive in the final 1:21 to set up kicker Adam Vinatieri's field goal.

A specially stamped ball, with the game's logo, is used for each Super Bowl.

ALL WRAPPED UP
Patriots defensive tackle Richard Seymour (93) and Willie McGinest (59) made life miserable for Rams quarterback Kurt Warner (13).

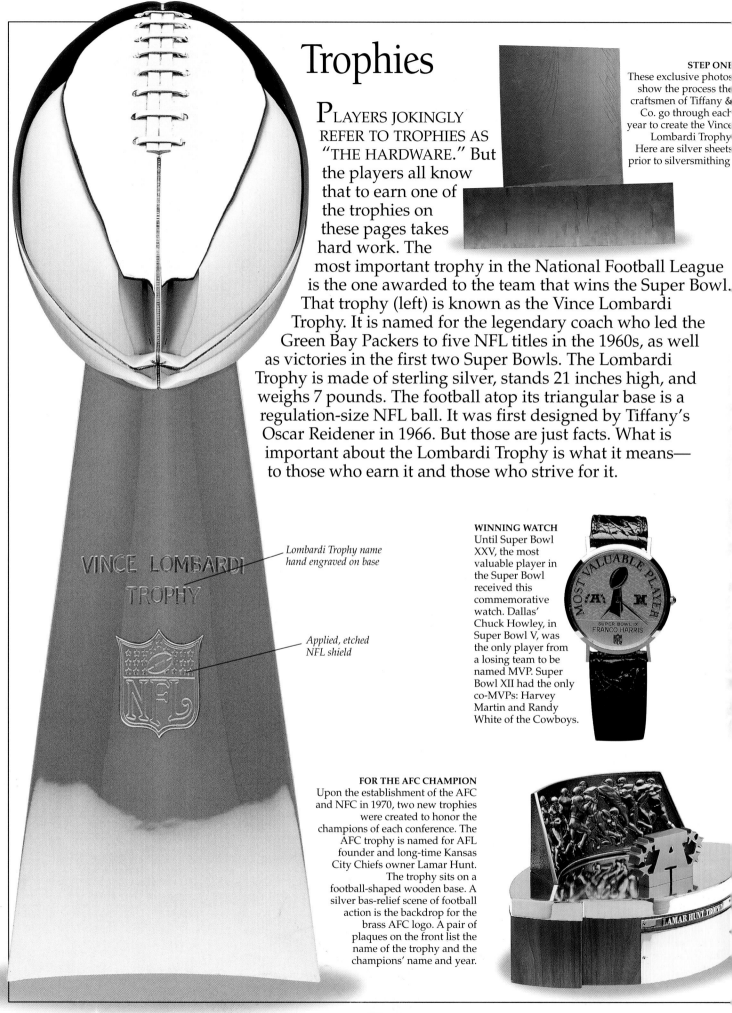

Trophies

Players jokingly refer to trophies as "the hardware." But the players all know that to earn one of the trophies on these pages takes hard work. The most important trophy in the National Football League is the one awarded to the team that wins the Super Bowl. That trophy (left) is known as the Vince Lombardi Trophy. It is named for the legendary coach who led the Green Bay Packers to five NFL titles in the 1960s, as well as victories in the first two Super Bowls. The Lombardi Trophy is made of sterling silver, stands 21 inches high, and weighs 7 pounds. The football atop its triangular base is a regulation-size NFL ball. It was first designed by Tiffany's Oscar Riedener in 1966. But those are just facts. What is important about the Lombardi Trophy is what it means— to those who earn it and those who strive for it.

STEP ONE
These exclusive photos show the process the craftsmen of Tiffany & Co. go through each year to create the Vince Lombardi Trophy. Here are silver sheets prior to silversmithing.

Lombardi Trophy name hand engraved on base

Applied, etched NFL shield

VINCE LOMBARDI TROPHY

WINNING WATCH
Until Super Bowl XXV, the most valuable player in the Super Bowl received this commemorative watch. Dallas' Chuck Howley, in Super Bowl V, was the only player from a losing team to be named MVP. Super Bowl XII had the only co-MVPs: Harvey Martin and Randy White of the Cowboys.

FOR THE AFC CHAMPION
Upon the establishment of the AFC and NFC in 1970, two new trophies were created to honor the champions of each conference. The AFC trophy is named for AFL founder and long-time Kansas City Chiefs owner Lamar Hunt. The trophy sits on a football-shaped wooden base. A silver bas-relief scene of football action is the backdrop for the brass AFC logo. A pair of plaques on the front list the name of the trophy and the champions' name and year.

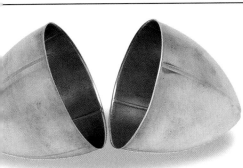

STEP TWO
The larger silver sheets are spun into two cones that form the football atop the base. This process takes about three days.

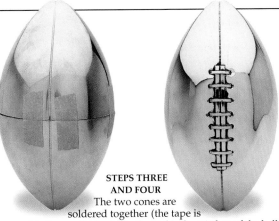

STEPS THREE AND FOUR
The two cones are soldered together (the tape is removed before polishing). On the right, the stitches of the ball have been applied by hand, and the seams have been "chased."

STEP FIVE
Another silver sheet is used to create the base. It is cut and shaped into three concave sections, then soldered together. Engraving is done before the football is attached. After a final polishing, the trophy is placed into a velvet-lined case and transported to the NFL for inspection. A backup trophy also is made.

DREAM COME TRUE
Hours in the weight room...days on the practice field...nights studying the playbook...and Sunday afternoons giving it all they've got. Why do NFL players do it? Simple: They do it so they can be like Reggie White (left) and the 1996 Packers and all the other Super Bowl winners. They put up with all the hard work and the sacrifice and the sweat for the chance to hold the Vince Lombardi Trophy and call themselves NFL champions.

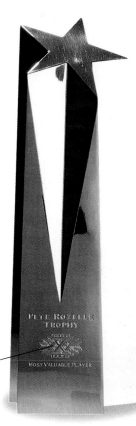

The hand-engraved inscription includes the name of the trophy, the Super Bowl logo, and the words "most valuable player."

FOR THE NFC CHAMPION
Similar in design to the AFC trophy, the NFC championship trophy is named for George Halas. Halas, an NFL founder and long-time owner of the Chicago Bears, was the only man to win NFL championships as a player, coach, and owner. He was inducted as a member of the inaugural class of the Pro Football Hall of Fame in 1963. Two years after Halas' death in 1983, his Chicago team hoisted the trophy bearing his name on their way to victory in Super Bowl XX.

Trophy awarded to the San Francisco 49ers after their victory in the 1984 NFC Championship Game.

MVP
Since Super Bowl XXV, the most valuable player of the Super Bowl has been awarded the Pete Rozelle Trophy, also created by Tiffany & Co. It is named for the NFL's former commissioner (1960-1989) and the man most responsible for pro football's status as America's number-one sport.

SUPER BOWL I
January 15, 1967
Champion:
Green Bay Packers

SUPER BOWL II
January 14, 1968
Champion:
Green Bay Packers

SUPER BOWL III
January 12, 1969
Champion:
New York Jets

SUPER BOWL IV
January 11, 1970
Champion:
Kansas City Chiefs

SUPER BOWL V
January 17, 1971
Champion:
Baltimore Colts

SUPER BOWL VI
January 16, 1972
Champion:
Dallas Cowboys

Super Bowl Rings

THEY PLAY FOR THE RINGS. Before Super Bowl XXXII, Broncos quarterback John Elway was asked if he would trade his individual achievements, created with years and years of hard work, for a Super Bowl ring. Without hesitating, he said, "In a heartbeat." Football is a team game, but the one individual prize that every NFL player dreams of is a Super Bowl ring. Each member of the Super Bowl-winning team receives the ring, as does the coaching staff and selected members of the front office. Each team designs its ring, and the NFL provides up to $5,000 for each of 125 rings for the winners.

SUPER BOWL XXXV
January 28, 2001
Champion:
Baltimore Ravens

SUPER BOWL XXXIV
January 30, 2000
Champion:
St. Louis Rams

SUPER BOWL XXXIII
January 31, 1999
Champion:
Denver Broncos

SUPER BOWL XXXII
January 25, 1998
Champion:
Denver Broncos

SUPER BOWL XXXI
January 26, 1997
Champion:
Green Bay Packers

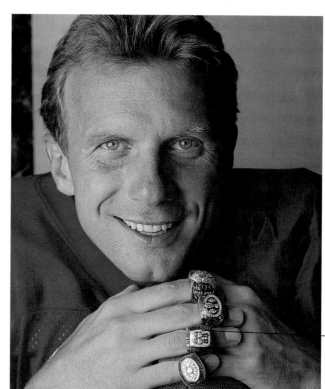

FOUR FOR FOUR
San Francisco quarterback Joe Montana displays his four Super Bowl rings. Montana, who also won three Super Bowl MVP awards, is one of many players with four rings. Defensive end Charles Haley holds the record with five. Haley played for San Francisco in Super Bowls XXIII and XXIV and Dallas in Super Bowls XXVII, XXVIII, and XXX.

Most players have their rings sized to fit on this finger, called the ring finger.

SUPER BOWL XXX
January 28, 1996
Champion:
Dallas Cowboys

SUPER BOWL XXIX
January 29, 1995
Champion:
San Francisco 49ers

SUPER BOWL XXVIII
January 30, 1994
Champion:
Dallas Cowboys

SUPER BOWL XXVII
January 31, 1993
Champion:
Dallas Cowboys

SUPER BOWL XXVI
January 26, 1992
Champion:
Washington Redskins

SUPER BOWL XXV
January 27, 1991
Champion:
New York Giants

SUPER BOWL VII
January 14, 1973
Champion:
Miami Dolphins

SUPER BOWL VIII
January 13, 1974
Champion:
Miami Dolphins

SUPER BOWL IX
January 12, 1975
Champion:
Pittsburgh Steelers

SUPER BOWL X
January 18, 1976
Champion:
Pittsburgh Steelers

SUPER BOWL XI
January 9, 1977
Champion:
Oakland Raiders

SUPER BOWL XII
January 15, 1978
Champion:
Dallas Cowboys

RED, WHITE, AND BLUE
This is the ring that Tom Brady dreamed of winning. Many compared the Patriots' quarterback to Cinderella, but her glass slipper disappeared at midnight…Brady's Super Bowl ring will last forever! The Patriots, who defeated the Rams 20-17 to win Super Bowl XXXVI, had their rings cast in 14-karat white gold. The top of the ring displays the Patriots logo, made from red garnet and blue sapphire, adorned by a Lombardi Trophy fashioned from diamonds and platinum.

Ring is encircled with 42 diamonds for the Patriots' 42 years in the NFL.

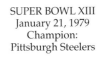

SUPER BOWL XIII
January 21, 1979
Champion:
Pittsburgh Steelers

SUPER BOWL XIV
January 20, 1980
Champion:
Pittsburgh Steelers

SUPER BOWL XV
January 25, 1981
Champion:
Oakland Raiders

SUPER BOWL XVI
January 24, 1982
Champion:
San Francisco 49ers

SUPER BOWL XVII
January 30, 1983
Champion:
Washington Redskins

Recipient's name and number appear along with American flag, the Patriots' 14-5 record, and the word "TEAM."

Two large football-shaped diamonds represent the Patriots' two previous Super Bowl trips.

Each ring contains 143 diamonds and weighs three ounces.

Cast in 14-karat white gold.

SUPER BOWL XVIII
January 22, 1984
Champion:
Los Angeles Raiders

SUPER BOWL XXIV
January 28, 1990
Champion:
San Francisco 49ers

SUPER BOWL XXIII
January 22, 1989
Champion:
San Francisco 49ers

SUPER BOWL XXII
January 31, 1988
Champion:
Washington Redskins

SUPER BOWL XXI
January 25, 1987
Champion:
New York Giants

SUPER BOWL XX
January 26, 1986
Champion:
Chicago Bears

SUPER BOWL XIX
January 20, 1985
Champion:
San Francisco 49ers

Amazing Super Bowl Plays

WOW, DID YOU SEE THAT? In the biggest game of all, players often come up with the biggest plays of their careers. Some of those plays are so big and so spectacular that they become a part of Super Bowl and NFL history. Of course, the importance of the Super Bowl magnifies what would be a less-important play if it occurred during the regular season. Long touchdowns runs occur nearly every week, especially by players such as Marcus Allen (right). But when that same play comes during the Super Bowl, with millions of people watching around the world, and with the NFL title at stake, the play becomes more than ordinary: It becomes extraordinary. Most of the memorable plays from Super Bowl games involve touchdowns. But two plays here involve seeming touchdowns that weren't.

Marcus Allen retired after the 1997 season with 145 touchdowns, second most all-time.

PICTURE PERFECT
All players, young and old, are taught to "wrap up" the player they are tackling. Rams linebacker Mike Jones (52) wrapped up Titans receiver Kevin Dyson less than a yard short of a touchdown to preserve the Rams' Super Bowl XXXIV victory.

RAIDERS

REDSKINS

Allen's path to the end zone.

ZIG-ZAG TO THE END ZONE
In Super Bowl XVIII, the Raiders' Marcus Allen made one of the best touchdown runs in Super Bowl history. Taking a handoff at the Raiders' 26-yard line, Allen first ran left—into a wall of Redskins. He reversed field and ran right, then cut back and took off up the middle. Allen dodged several tacklers and then won a sprint to the end zone. The record run helped the Raiders defeat the Redskins 38-9, and Allen was named the game's MVP.

IT'S A RUN...NO, IT'S A PASS
Sometimes the unexpected play becomes the big one. In Super Bowl XIV, Rams running back Lawrence McCutcheon (30) took a handoff and started to run. Suddenly, he stopped and threw a 24-yard touchdown pass to Ron Smith that gave the Rams a 19-17 lead over Pittsburgh. But the surprise "halfback-option" play wasn't enough; the Steelers came back to defeat the Rams.

A player who receives a handoff can then make a forward pass from behind the line of scrimmage.

GARO'S GOOF

One of the most famous plays in Super Bowl history also was one of the goofiest. In Super Bowl VII, Miami led Washington 14-0 when Dolphins kicker Garo Yepremian (1) attempted a field goal. The kick was blocked (left), and Garo, a fine kicker but a football novice, chased after the ball (center), picked it up, and tried to pass it (right). He bobbled the ball and the Redskins' Mike Bass caught it in midair and returned it for a touchdown.

Brown had 54 interceptions in his 16-year, Hall of Fame career.

ONE THAT WASN'T

Perhaps the biggest miss in Super Bowl history came in Super Bowl XIII when Dallas tight end Jackie Smith dropped a sure touchdown catch in the third quarter of a game that Dallas lost to Pittsburgh.

Smith played 16 seasons in the NFL. He was elected to the Pro Football Hall of Fame in 1994.

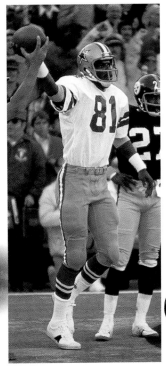

HIS ONE AND ONLY

Super Bowl X was nearly over and the Cowboys trailed the Steelers 21-7. But there was enough time for Dallas receiver Percy Howard to become the answer to this trivia question: What player caught a touchdown pass in the Super Bowl for the only NFL reception of his career?

AN ASSIST FROM VIDEO

Green Bay kick returner Desmond Howard (81) had a little help as he neared the end zone during this record 99-yard kickoff-return touchdown in Super Bowl XXXI. He looked up at the giant video screen in the end zone to see how close pursuing Patriots were.

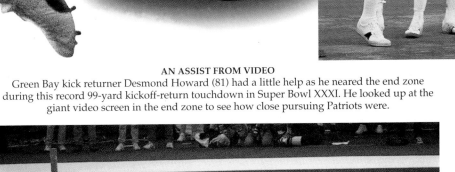

SILVER, BLACK, AND BROWN

Raiders cornerback Willie Brown set a Super Bowl record with his game-clinching 75-yard interception return for a touchdown in Super Bowl XI. The Raiders defeated the Vikings 32-14, the Raiders' first NFL championship.

Super Bowl Records

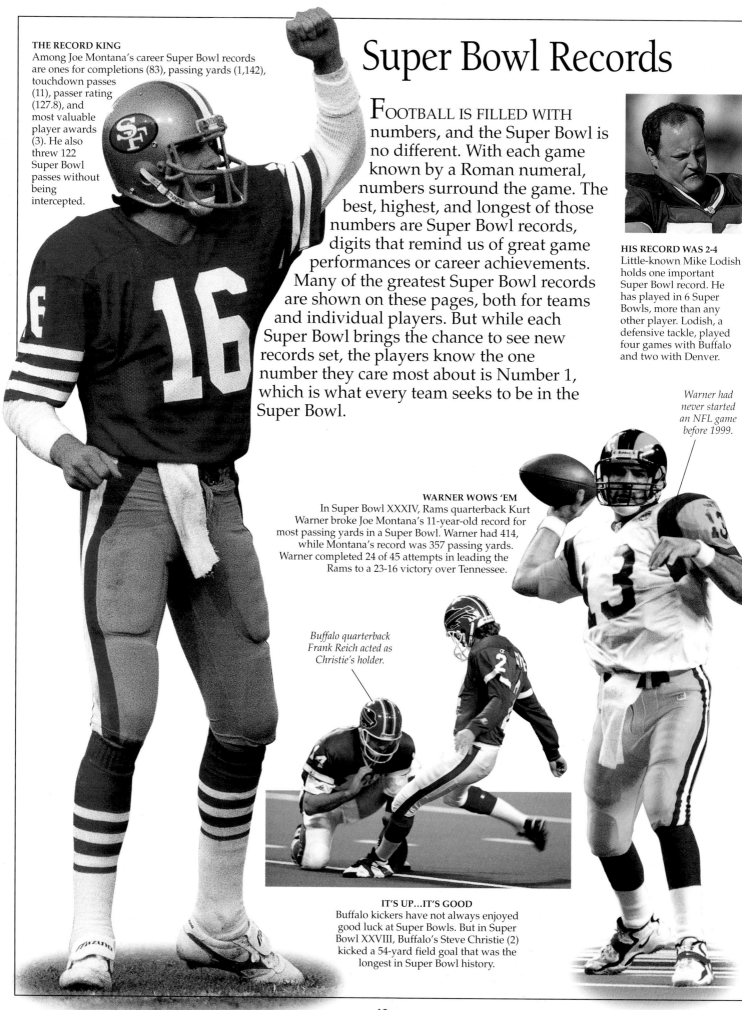

THE RECORD KING
Among Joe Montana's career Super Bowl records are ones for completions (83), passing yards (1,142), touchdown passes (11), passer rating (127.8), and most valuable player awards (3). He also threw 122 Super Bowl passes without being intercepted.

FOOTBALL IS FILLED WITH numbers, and the Super Bowl is no different. With each game known by a Roman numeral, numbers surround the game. The best, highest, and longest of those numbers are Super Bowl records, digits that remind us of great game performances or career achievements. Many of the greatest Super Bowl records are shown on these pages, both for teams and individual players. But while each Super Bowl brings the chance to see new records set, the players know the one number they care most about is Number 1, which is what every team seeks to be in the Super Bowl.

HIS RECORD WAS 2-4
Little-known Mike Lodish holds one important Super Bowl record. He has played in 6 Super Bowls, more than any other player. Lodish, a defensive tackle, played four games with Buffalo and two with Denver.

Warner had never started an NFL game before 1999.

WARNER WOWS 'EM
In Super Bowl XXXIV, Rams quarterback Kurt Warner broke Joe Montana's 11-year-old record for most passing yards in a Super Bowl. Warner had 414, while Montana's record was 357 passing yards. Warner completed 24 of 45 attempts in leading the Rams to a 23-16 victory over Tennessee.

Buffalo quarterback Frank Reich acted as Christie's holder.

IT'S UP...IT'S GOOD
Buffalo kickers have not always enjoyed good luck at Super Bowls. But in Super Bowl XXVIII, Buffalo's Steve Christie (2) kicked a 54-yard field goal that was the longest in Super Bowl history.

OTHER SUPER BOWL RECORDS

MOST FIELD GOALS, CAREER
5
Ray Wersching, San Francisco

•

LONGEST RUN FROM SCRIMMAGE
74 yards
Marcus Allen, L.A. Raiders,
Super Bowl XVIII

•

HIGHEST COMPLETION
PERCENTAGE, CAREER
70.0
Troy Aikman, Dallas

•

MOST PASSES ATTEMPTED, CAREER
152
John Elway, Denver

•

MOST TOUCHDOWN PASSES, GAME
6
Steve Young, San Francisco,
Super Bowl XXIX

•

PUNT RETURNS, HIGHEST AVERAGE,
CAREER
15.7
John Taylor, San Francisco

•

KICKOFF RETURNS, HIGHEST
AVERAGE, CAREER
42.0
Tim Dwight, Atlanta

•

MOST INTERCEPTIONS, CAREER
3
Chuck Howley, Dallas
Rod Martin, Oakland
Larry Brown, Dallas

•

MOST SACKS, CAREER
4½
Charles Haley, San Francisco/Dallas

•

MOST SACKS, GAME
3
Reggie White, Green Bay,
Super Bowl XXXI

•

LONGEST FUMBLE RETURN
64
Leon Lett, Dallas, Super Bowl XXVII

•

LONGEST PASS COMPLETION
81
Brett Favre to Antonio Freeman, Green Bay,
Super Bowl XXXI (TD)

FRANCO RULES!
Many of the NFL's greatest running backs have shown their stuff in Super Bowls, but none as well as Pittsburgh's Franco Harris. In four Super Bowl victories, he ran the ball a record 101 times for a record 354 rushing yards. Harris was the MVP of Super Bowl IX.

THE HEAD MAN
In 1969, Chuck Noll became head coach of the Pittsburgh Steelers, a team that had finished 2-11-1 the year before and hadn't had a winning season since 1963. But just five years later, Noll led the Steelers to the first of what would become four Super Bowl titles in six years. He holds the record for most Super Bowl victories by a head coach.

Headset with microphone connects head coach to coaches in the press box above the field.

THE TOUCHDOWN MACHINE
If the name of the game in football is scoring, then Jerry Rice is the best ever. The 49ers' wide receiver not only is the NFL's all-time leader in career touchdowns, but also is the Super Bowl record holder with 8 career touchdowns.

AMERICA'S TEAM
No team has appeared in the Super Bowl more often than the Dallas Cowboys. The club has played in eight of the games, winning five (which ties San Francisco for most victories). Bob Lilly (74), a Hall of Fame defensive tackle, played in two Super Bowls for the Cowboys.

ALL THE WAY BACK
Some Super Bowl records involve "firsts." Sixteen Super Bowls had been played before Miami's Fulton Walker became the first player to return a kickoff for a touchdown. Walker's 98-yard return wasn't enough, however, to stop the Redskins from defeating the Dolphins in Super Bowl XVII.

Super Bowl Coaches

IF THE SUPER BOWL IS A HURRICANE OF ACTIVITY, then the head coaches are at the eye of that hurricane. During Super Week, they must not only plan for the biggest game of their careers, they must face the world's media. Head coaches take part in media sessions every day of the week, often answering the same questions many times. On Super Bowl Sunday, facing enormous pressure, the coaches call the plays, choose the players to run those plays, and then face the consequences. Once the game begins, they engage in a 60-minute chess match, with moves and countermoves. And if their plan is successful, the coaches take a joyous trip off the field on the shoulders of their players.

THE WIZARD OF WASHINGTON
Joe Gibbs was the head coach of Washington from 1981-1992, leading the Redskins to Super Bowl championships in XVII, XXII, and XXVI. Gibbs was not only a great play caller and organizer, but a master motivator who got the most out of his players. Gibbs retired following the Redskins' third title and now is involved in auto racing.

WALSH THE WINNER
Bill Walsh led the San Francisco 49ers to Super Bowl championships in XVI, XIX, and XXIII. The team he helped create also won Super Bowl XXIV under the direction of head coach George Seifert. Walsh is regarded as one of the great offensive football minds of all time.

Walsh carefully scripted his team's first 15-20 plays each game.

THE CHIEF OF THE CHIEFS
Hank Stram not only led the Kansas City Chiefs to their only Super Bowl title, he became a permanent part of Super Bowl history. He wore a microphone during the game. His enthusiastic chatter was captured in a famous movie made by NFL Films that often is replayed at Super Bowl time.

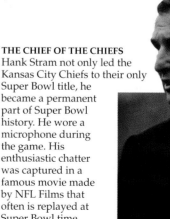

ONE BIG, BAD BEAR
Chicago Bears coach Mike Ditka was as tough as his players. His fierce style helped create the Super Bowl XX-champion Bears, one of the most dominant teams in NFL history.

MR. SUPER BOWL
Dan Reeves has participated in nine Super Bowls, more than any other person. He has taken part in Super Bowls as a player for the Dallas Cowboys, as an assistant coach for Dallas, and as head coach of the Atlanta Falcons (left) and Denver Broncos.

GOING FOR TWO
Bill Parcells (below), Dan Reeves, and Don Shula are the only coaches to lead two different teams to berths in the Super Bowl. Parcells won Super Bowls XXI and XXV with the New York Giants, using a clock-eating ground game of his design. His New England Patriots team lost Super Bowl XXXI to Green Bay.

TOM TERRIFIC
Tom Flores was the first person to earn Super Bowl rings as a player, assistant coach, and head coach. He was a backup quarterback for Kansas City (IV), an assistant for the Oakland Raiders (XI), and head coach for the Raiders in XV and XVIII. Here he rides off the field after winning Super Bowl XVIII.

CLOSE, BUT NO CIGAR
Minnesota's Bud Grant (left) and Buffalo's Marv Levy share an unfortunate distinction. Both men led their teams to four Super Bowls…and both men's teams lost four Super Bowls. They also share another distinction—both are in the Pro Football Hall of Fame.

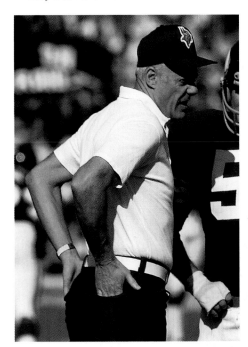

Pregame Show

FLYING PIGSKIN
This Army parachutist delivered the official game ball at Super Bowl XVII.

THE SUPER BOWL SPECTACLE DOESN'T wait for kickoff to begin. The Pregame Show always gets the day off to an entertaining beginning. At the first Super Bowls, the shows weren't much more than a marching band or some recorded music. Today, the shows are field-spanning extravaganzas with dancers, superstar singers and performers, fireworks, and more. Also part of the pregame festivities are the National Anthem, the coin toss (to determine which team kicks off and which receives), and the introduction of the players. Each team's starting offense or defense is introduced and sprints onto the field through a tunnel of cheerleaders and teammates. Many players call the moment when they finally take the field for a Super Bowl one of the highlights of their careers.

DANCE, DANCE, DANCE
Every Super Bowl Pregame Show includes hundreds of dancers, like these from XXVII.

PREGAME HIGHLIGHT
The highlight of every Pregame Show held in an outdoor stadium always is the flyover by U.S. military jets. Roaring overhead, the jets zoom over the stadium at the end of the National Anthem (as they do here at Super Bowl XXXII). Their ear-rattling appearance always gets the game off to a rousing beginning.

ON THEIR FEET
For Super Bowl XXV, during the Persian Gulf War, Whitney Houston created a lasting memory with her inspiring version of the National Anthem.

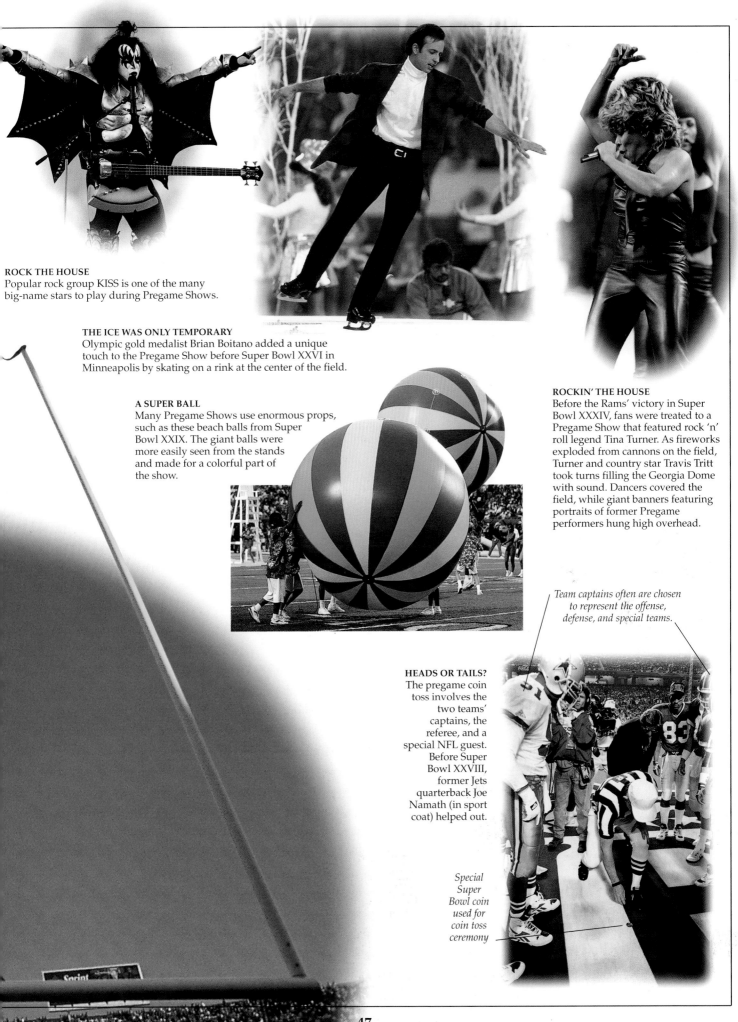

ROCK THE HOUSE
Popular rock group KISS is one of the many big-name stars to play during Pregame Shows.

THE ICE WAS ONLY TEMPORARY
Olympic gold medalist Brian Boitano added a unique touch to the Pregame Show before Super Bowl XXVI in Minneapolis by skating on a rink at the center of the field.

A SUPER BALL
Many Pregame Shows use enormous props, such as these beach balls from Super Bowl XXIX. The giant balls were more easily seen from the stands and made for a colorful part of the show.

ROCKIN' THE HOUSE
Before the Rams' victory in Super Bowl XXXIV, fans were treated to a Pregame Show that featured rock 'n' roll legend Tina Turner. As fireworks exploded from cannons on the field, Turner and country star Travis Tritt took turns filling the Georgia Dome with sound. Dancers covered the field, while giant banners featuring portraits of former Pregame performers hung high overhead.

Team captains often are chosen to represent the offense, defense, and special teams.

HEADS OR TAILS?
The pregame coin toss involves the two teams' captains, the referee, and a special NFL guest. Before Super Bowl XXVIII, former Jets quarterback Joe Namath (in sport coat) helped out.

Special Super Bowl coin used for coin toss ceremony

Halftime Show

Fans sometimes perform card stunts during the show.

THERE ARE TWO BIG SHOWS ON Super Bowl Sunday. One begins when the game kicks off. The other begins when the first half ends. That's when the Super Bowl Halftime Show takes over while the players take a rest. In the past decade, the Halftime Show has become almost as big a part of Super Sunday as the game. Fans in the stadium and watching at home look forward to seeing some of the most popular entertainers in the world perform music ranging from pop to jazz to soul to rhythm and blues. Everyone from Michael Jackson to Shania Twain, from Phil Collins to *NSYNC, and from Stevie Wonder to U2 have graced the stage of a Super Bowl Halftime Show extravagana. Stay tuned for next year's performance.

STAR POWER
The Halftime Show can bring stars from different generations on the same stage, as was the case at Super Bowl XXXV with Britney Spears and Steven Tyler of Aerosmith (left).

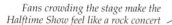

Fans crowding the stage make the Halftime Show feel like a rock concert

THE 'OLD' DAYS
Before the glitz and glamour of the Halftime Show caught up to the enormity of the game, the show often was as simple as cheerleaders riding on NFL helmet-covered cars, accompanied by college marching bands.

TRIBUTE
Rock supergroup U2 remembered the victims of 9/11 with an emotional performance at Super Bowl XXXVI. The Irish band capped the mini-concert by performing "Where the Streets Have No Name" while the names of the victims scrolled behind them (above). The band's members, from left to right: guitarist The Edge, lead singer Bono, drummer Larry Mullen, and bassist Adam Clayton.

MUSICAL GUMBO
Super Bowl XXXI in New Orleans featured the best in blues, soul, rock, and R&B together on stage, along with a spectacular light and dance show.

ROCKETTES
The Super Bowl XXII Halftime Show included the Radio City Rockettes.

TOP ARTISTS
The Super Bowl Halftime Show attracts the industry's best and most glamorous stars, including singer Shania Twain at Super Bowl XXXVII.

HARD WORKING SOUL MAN
Superstar soul singer James Brown was a vision in red when he headlined the show at Super Bowl XXXI. He was joined by ZZ Top and the Blues Brothers.

UP, UP, AND AWAY
Diana Ross boards her ride home at the conclusion of her Super Bowl XXX performance. Ross was still singing as the helicopter landed on the stage and whisked her away.

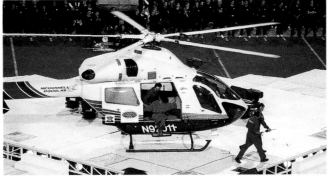

The NFL Experience

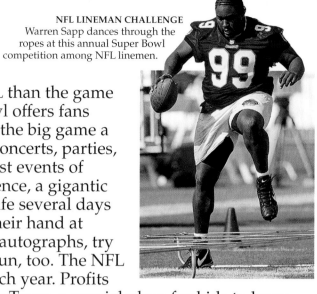

NFL LINEMAN CHALLENGE
Warren Sapp dances through the ropes at this annual Super Bowl competition among NFL linemen.

THERE'S MORE TO THE SUPER BOWL than the game on Sunday. Each year, the Super Bowl offers fans dozens of ways to make their trip to the big game a special one. The host cities sponsor concerts, parties, festivals, and more. One of the biggest events of Super Bowl Week is the NFL Experience, a gigantic football theme park that springs to life several days before the game. Kids can play on indoor fields, try their hand at interactive football games, meet NFL players and get autographs, try on NFL equipment, and lots more. Parents can have fun, too. The NFL Experience attracts several hundred thousand fans each year. Profits from the event help support the NFL Youth Education Town, a special place for kids to learn and play that is set up permanently in each Super Bowl city.

SIGN HERE, PLEASE
At the annual Super Bowl Youth Clinic, NFL players show kids how to pass, run, and catch. They also talk about staying in school and staying off drugs. Of course, they also enjoy signing a lot of autographs, too.

ANOTHER KIND OF HELMET
At Ride Like a Pro, kids learn the importance of bike safety helmets from NFL players and local police officers.

FEET, FEET, FEET!
Kids at the NFL Experience try their hand—and feet—at games that test their football skills, such as this obstacle course race.

Padded pylons make for great obstacles at this NFL Experience event.

Padded sidewalls help keep kids safe as they run through the course.

See what it would be like to live inside a football at this exhibit.

Kids try to kick a field goal through these goal posts.

Several tents offer exhibits of NFL memorabilia.

Dive over this wall onto an air-filled pad to score a touchdown.

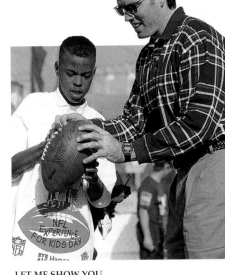

LET ME SHOW YOU
Tennessee Titans quarterback Neil O'Donnell shows a young fan how to throw a spiral. Many NFL players visit the NFL Experience.

Artificial turf is used to make several fields.

In this game, kids try to see who can put on an NFL uniform in the fastest time.

THAT'S A BIG BEAR
Not only NFL stars visit the NFL Experience to meet fans. NFL team mascots often drop by to say hello and pose for pictures. This mascot is for the Chicago Bears.

A BIG SPREAD
The NFL Experience has been held since Super Bowl XXVI. In some cities, it is held outdoors on land near the Super Bowl stadium. In others, the event is held inside an enormous building, such as a convention center.

PUT ME IN, COACH!
Visitors can pretend they've made the team by posing inside these life-sized NFL uniforms. Uniforms from every NFL team are available for fans to "wear."

This is the symbol for NFL kids' programs.

GOOD PASS!
This young player shows good form in making a pass during a special contest held at the NFL Experience before Super Bowl XXXII.

Super Bowl Collectibles

IF A SUPER BOWL LOGO will fit on it, you can be sure that someone will make it. What is "it"? A Super Bowl souvenir. Fans attending the game will take home football memories to last a lifetime, while fans around the world will remember watching the game on TV. But whether they go to the game or to the living room, fans are looking for more than memories to take away from the Super Bowl. That is where the souvenir and collectible makers of the world come in. Every imaginable product is available as a souvenir of the Super Bowl. These pages illustrate only a tiny fraction of the many things that fans buy to make the game part of their lives. Fans can wear the Super Bowl, eat on the Super Bowl, read the Super Bowl, decorate with the Super Bowl, play golf with the Super Bowl, and much, much more.

ON SALE HERE!
Fans in the Super Bowl host city have the best access to dozens of Super Bowl souvenirs, such as at this display at Super Bowl XXII. Some Super Bowl merchandise includes the two teams' logos; all of those items must be made in a very short time, after the teams qualify.

PIN IT ON
Metal pins (below and on following pages) are fun, easy to collect, and come in an enormous variety of styles and designs.

Bumper stickers for each team

Pins for the game and for each team

Pennant with teams, game, and date

Special media pin awarded to veteran Super Bowl reporters.

Super Bowl XXIV pin features Mississippi riverboat design.

Another special pin from Super Bowl XXV.

Media pin from Super Bowl XXXI features jazz musician.

Souvenir salesmen usually are local people earning extra money during Super Week.

POPULAR PROGRAM
The Official Super Bowl Game Program (right and below) always is one of the most popular collectibles available to fans. The program has stories about past games and NFL stars, as well as Super Bowl records, results from the previous season, and lineups, rosters, and scouting reports for the two Super Bowl teams.

Super Bowl XXXII Game Program

Stand set up outside stadium to sell programs.

GOTTA HAVE HATS
These hats were designed like baseball caps, but they and dozens like them are sold to football fans at Super Bowls. Souvenir caps are among the most-worn items by fans attending Super Bowls. Many companies produce hats in a variety of designs and colors.

Super Bowl XX Game Program

THE SILVER PAGES
NFL Publishing produced this special commemorative Super Bowl book to honor the game's 25th anniversary in 1991. The story of each game featured a gatefold illustration of action scenes of the game's heroes.

Illustration used all the NFL team helmet logos.

Super Bowl II Game Program

ABC Sports issued its own pin at Super Bowl XIX.

A pin from a set given only to veteran Super Bowl writers.

NFL sponsors make pins, too; this is from Super Bowl XX.

Super Bowl XX pin in the shape of the Lombardi Trophy.

Super Bowl Collectibles

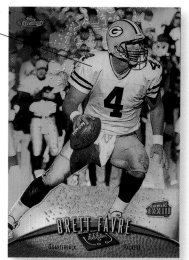

Green Bay quarterback Brett Favre

While hundreds of collectibles are available to fans, some of those items are more valuable than others. Scarcity determines a collectible's value, along with the meaningfulness of the item to the buyer. A Jets' fan, for instance, will be more interested in Super Bowl III memorabilia than the fan of another team. Special limited-edition items also increase in value over time. One of the attractions at the NFL Experience each year is the giant Super Bowl Card Show, a massive market for Super Bowl, football, and sports cards, collectibles, and, well, stuff. The Super Bowl is not only the biggest game in town… it's the biggest marketplace.

SOUVENIR PIGSKIN
The official Super Bowl football made by Wilson is stamped in gold with the game's logo. After the game, fans also can buy a ball with the score of the game stamped on it.

FOR THE KIDS
Souvenirs for all ages are available at the Super Bowl. These teddy bears and squishy foam footballs are made for toddlers. T-shirts and other clothing all come in kids' sizes, too. More souvenirs have been made for children in recent seasons than in years past as the Super Bowl has grown in popularity.

MORE THAN CARDBOARD
Football cards are a big hit with collectors. This Super Bowl XXXIII set used holograms to create a special look at past Super Bowl heroes.

FORE!
Different game, different kind of ball. Football fans took their Super Bowl memories to the golf course with this set of golf balls from Super Bowl XXI.

Pins are cast in metal from molds.

This pin was made using a process similar to cloisonné.

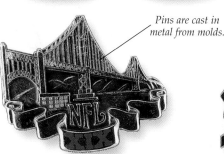

This Super Bowl XIX pin features the Golden Gate Bridge.

Super Bowl XXI was held at the Rose Bowl stadium.

This Super Bowl XX pin doubled as a key chain.

Super Bowl XXV got special treatment on this pin.

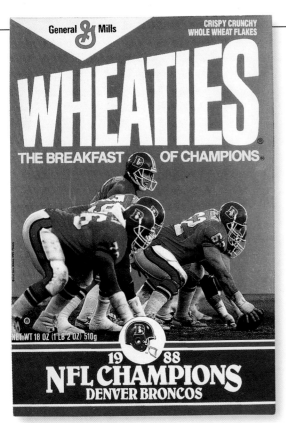

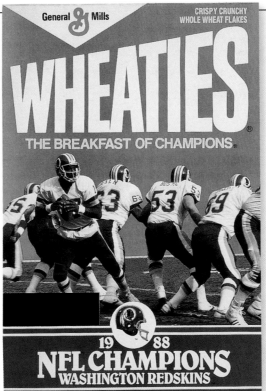

ONLY ONE WAS A WINNER
Many Super Bowl souvenirs are not sold until after the game is over, to celebrate and honor the champion. These cereal boxes were made before Super Bowl XXII, and were ready to go to stores depending on which team won. The Redskins' version was the only one that hit store shelves. The Broncos' version became a rare collectible.

Collectors' card came with action figure.

CHEERS!
All sorts of cups, glasses, and mugs are sold at the Super Bowl, including the ceramic mugs from Super Bowl VI (top, featuring a newspaper page about the game) and Super Bowl XXIX, and the blue glass version from Super Bowl XXXIV. Fans can save them for use at next year's Super Bowl party.

BALLOT
SUPER BOWL XXXVI SITE

_____ NEW ORLEANS

_____ SAN DIEGO

CASTING A VOTE
NFL owners used cards like this one—a rarely seen piece of memorabilia—to decide what city would play host to Super Bowl XXXVI, to be played in January 2002. The winner? New Orleans, home to eight previous Super Bowls.

IT'S NOT A DOLL...
It's an action figure. These collectible figures were sold at Super Bowl XXXIII. Many of the NFL's top players were turned into moveable plastic statues.

The Super Bowl XIX champions were honored with this pin.

Football goalposts adorned this Super Bowl XXIII pin.

The NFLPA issued this pin for Super Bowl XX.

Miami palm trees decorated this Super Bowl XXIII pin.

The Media

ONE OF THE MOST IMPORTANT REASONS the Super Bowl has become such an enormous event is the media. Writers, reporters, photographers, cameramen, announcers, and Web site creators from around the world converge on the Super Bowl city each year by the thousands. These men and women tell the stories of the teams, the players, and the game to billions of people around the world. At Super Bowl XXXIV, more than 3,500 journalists received credentials to cover the game, sending their stories back to more than 180 countries.

Earphone connects announcer to control booth.

A PLAYER AND HIS FORMER COACH
Frank Gifford (with microphone, left) was one of the CBS announcers for Super Bowl I. Here he interviews Packers coach Vince Lombardi. Gifford played for the Giants in the 1950s, when Lombardi was an assistant coach with the team. Gifford is one of many former NFL players who became broadcasters after retiring.

TAKING YOU TO THE HUDDLE
Television cameras help fans get right in the middle of the action at Super Bowls. During Super Bowl XXIII, this cameraman gave fans an up-close look at the 49ers' pregame gathering. At Super Bowl XXXIV, ABC used 40 cameras to cover the game.

LOOK! UP IN THE SKY!
Several blimps fly above the Super Bowl to give TV viewers a birds-eye view of the stadium.

Pilots ride in the gondola.

SAY CHEESE!
The enormous number of press people at the game makes the postgame scene on the field quite a crowded one. Here, Packers coach Mike Holmgren rides his players' shoulders after winning Super Bowl XXXI while dozens of photographers rush in to capture the magic moment.

EVERYBODY WATCHES
Even busy world leaders take time out to watch the Super Bowl. President Bill Clinton (center) was joined by Texas Gov. Ann Richards and New York Gov. Mario Cuomo for Super Bowl XXVIII. Chelsea Clinton is sitting in front.

CROWDED HOUSE
More than 300 photographers line the sidelines of the Super Bowl, taking hundreds of thousands of photographs before, during, and after the game. Most of them use special long lenses to get deep into the action.

ACE SHOOTERS
The best sports photographers in the world cover the Super Bowl. They come to the game with several cameras and lenses and other equipment to do their job.

Team helmet logos

COMMUNICATIONS
To help reporters get their stories out, the NFL provides them with lots of help in the press box, such as special phones like this one from Super Bowl XX.

One of two different cameras

Light meter

Former Raiders coach John Madden

UP IN THE BOOTH
Super Bowl announcers usually include an expert analyst and a broadcaster who calls the play-by-play.

Veteran play-by-play man Pat Summerall

Field pass

Super Stadiums

Tulane Stadium in New Orleans, on the campus of Tulane University, was the site of three Super Bowls, including IX.

THE GAME IS CERTAINLY SUPER, but why "Bowl"? That part of the Super Bowl's name comes from football stadiums, the earliest of which were shaped like deep bowls, such as the Yale Bowl in Connecticut. Important postseason college games began to be called "Bowls" after the shape of the stadium. So when it came time to name the NFL's championship game, the "Bowl" name just fit into football tradition. As for the Super Bowl stadiums, 15 different stadiums hosted the first 37 Super Bowls. These ranged from indoor stadiums, such as the Louisiana Superdome in New Orleans, to enormous open-air arenas, such as the Rose Bowl in Pasadena. Super Bowl stadiums are carefully prepared to be in tip-top condition for the big game. Not only are they decorated from top to bottom, new grass often is put on the field just before the game.

This fleet of buses in Miami for Super Bowl XIII helped nearly 80,000 people attend the game in the Orange Bowl.

BIG CROWDS
Every Super Bowl but the first one has been a sellout. The largest crowd ever to watch a Super Bowl was at Super Bowl XIV, when 103,985 people filled the Rose Bowl in Pasadena, California. Every Super Bowl stadium is ringed with hundreds of buses that bring fans from around the nation.

The roof of the Pontiac Silverdome is made of special heavy-duty fabric supported by rigid beams and air pressure.

Super Bowl stadium scoreboards keep fans entertained between plays and provide a wealth of information.

INDOOR ATTRACTION
The Pontiac Silverdome in Pontiac, Michigan, played host to Super Bowl XVI, including this college marching band during the pregame ceremonies. Nine Super Bowls have been played at four indoor stadiums: the Silverdome, the Louisiana Superdome, the Georgia Dome, and the Minneapolis Metrodome.

Circular ramps at Miami's Pro Player Stadium

SUPER CITIES
New Orleans has hosted a record nine Super Bowls, while Miami has hosted the game eight times. Miami has had games at Pro Player Stadium (left), also known as Joe Robbie Stadium, as well as at the Orange Bowl.

A SUPER STADIUM SCENE
This overhead view of the Rose Bowl in Pasadena, California, during Super Bowl XXVII gives a spectacular panoramic view of Super Sunday. Although the game is held in January, weather rarely has been a big problem at the Super Bowl. The NFL mainly chooses cities with pleasant January weather, which is appreciated by both players and fans.

Blimps hover above every outdoor Super Bowl stadium to provide television viewers with a birds-eye view.

AN ENORMOUS TAILGATE PARTY
Before every Super Bowl, the NFL holds one of the biggest tailgate parties in the world. Tailgate parties are traditional pregame festivities held in the stadium parking lot. At the Super Bowl, 20,000 people enjoy a feast and great music before heading to the enty gates.

FANS GET IN THE ACT
At Super Bowl XXVII, the stadium was part of the show. At halftime, singing star Michael Jackson put on a showstopping performance. For part of the show, the 98,374 people in the stands flipped colored cards to create a stadium-spanning tableau of pictures of children from around the world.

Site of the "satellite city" that TV networks from around the world bring in to broadcast the Super Bowl.

The Super Bowl stadium end zones are specially painted with team colors of the participants.

The Rose Bowl has been the site of five Super Bowls, and is home to college football's oldest postseason bowl game.

Crowds stream into the stadium through a gauntlet of souvenir stands, food stands, and celebrating fans.

Road to the Super Bowl

SUPER BOWL TEAMS are determined during the NFL playoffs, which begin the weekend after the regular season ends. Twelve teams earn playoff spots, six from the AFC and six from the NFC. The four division champions from each conference make the playoffs, while two wild-card teams (the runner-up teams with best records) from each conference also reach the postseason. Following the wild-card playoffs are the divisional playoffs and then the conference championship games, with the winner advancing to the Super Bowl. The NFL playoffs often are among the most exciting games of the season…and the most important. Here are some of their stories.

Titans receiver Kevin Dyson had never before run the lateral play on which he scored.

WHO GOT IT?
A berth in Super Bowl XXX was determined on this play in the 1995 AFC Championship Game. If Colts receiver Aaron Bailey (in white) had made this catch, his team would have made the Super Bowl. Sadly for Colts fans, he didn't.

'THE MUSIC CITY MIRACLE'
In a 1999 wild-card playoff game, Tennessee trailed Buffalo 16-15 with only 16 seconds remaining. The Titans received the Bills' kickoff and ran a trick play called "Home Run Throwback." Lorenzo Neal fielded the ball and handed off to Frank Wycheck, who threw back across the field to Kevin Dyson (87), who ran 75 yards for a touchdown. It was one of the most amazing endings to a game in NFL history and helped boost the Titans to their first Super Bowl berth.

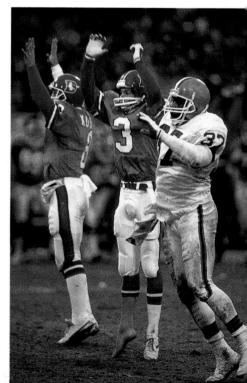

'THE DRIVE'
The Broncos trailed the Browns 20-13 with five minutes remaining in the 1986 AFC Championship Game. Then Denver quarterback John Elway led the Broncos on one of the greatest clutch marches in NFL playoff history. Elway ended the 98-yard drive with a touchdown pass to Mark Jackson with 37 seconds remaining to tie the score. In overtime, Rich Karlis (3), a barefoot kicker, nailed a 33-yard field goal that sent Denver to Super Bowl XXI.

HE GAVE IT ALL HE HAD
The San Diego Chargers' 41-38 overtime victory over Miami in the 1981 playoffs has been called one of the greatest games ever. The all-out effort of Chargers tight end Kellen Winslow (80) remains an inspiration.

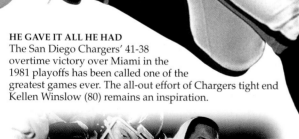

Ball deflected backward | Harris catches at the X | Harris

Disbelieving Raiders player gets the bad news.

'THE IMMACULATE RECEPTION'

This play from a 1972 AFC playoff game recently was voted the greatest play of the century by NFL fans. On the play, Pittsburgh's Franco Harris caught a pass that had been deflected backward, and Harris ran to the end zone to complete a 60-yard touchdown pass play to give the Steelers their first playoff win ever.

COMEBACK!

Early in the third quarter of an 1992 AFC playoff game, the Buffalo Bills trailed the Houston Oilers 35-3. No problem: Bills quarterback Frank Reich (14) led Buffalo to the greatest comeback in playoff history— the Bills won 41-38 in overtime.

Handwarmer used in cold weather

George Halas Trophy for NFC championship

'THE CATCH'

San Francisco's Dwight Clark (87) prepares to spike the ball after his spectacular game-winning catch in the 1981 NFC Championship Game. The fingertip grab, on a 6-yard pass from Joe Montana, put the 49ers in their first Super Bowl.

ONE MORE TO PLAY

St. Louis quarterback Kurt Warner passed 30 yards to Ricky Proehl for a touchdown to clinch the Rams' 1999 NFC title. But while this trophy was nice, the Rams got the prize they really wanted by winning Super Bowl XXXIV.

Super Bowl XXXVII

THE TAMPA BAY BUCCANEERS made their first Super Bowl appearance one to remember. Armed with the NFL's top-ranked defense—and facing the number-one offense—they forced 5 interceptions, returning 3 for touchdowns, to stun the favored Oakland Raiders 48-21. Buccaneers coach Jon Gruden, who once coached the Raiders, had his new team ready for every offensive trick his old team attempted. In the end, Raiders quarterback Rich Gannon, the NFL's MVP for the 2002 season, suffered his worst performance of the season. Meanwhile, the less-heralded Buccaneers, led by Brad Johnson, moved both on the ground and through the air. They totaled 365 yards and controlled possession for more than 37 minutes.

PRESSURE COOKER
Warren Sapp (99) and the Buccaneers put constant pressure on quarterback Rich Gannon (12), collecting 5 sacks and forcing numerous hurried passes.

SECRET WEAPON
Wide receiver Joe Jurevicius, who was not a member of the starting offense, came in off the bench to make 4 catches for a game-high 78 yards.

Receivers often wear a towel to dry their hands.

MR. COOL
Quarterback Brad Johnson, never known as a flamboyant sort, coolly directed 5 scoring drives, passing for 215 yards and 2 touchdowns.

PREGAME PERFORMER
Celine Dion, who sang "God Bless America," was among the entertainers to appear in a star-studded Pregame Show.

FAMILIAR FACE
Raiders wide receiver Jerry Rice (80), no stranger to the NFL's biggest game, extended his own record with an eighth career Super Bowl touchdown reception.

MVP
Buccaneers safety Dexter Jackson (34) was named the game's most valuable player after intercepting 2 passes in the first half. He became only the third defensive back to claim the honor. The others were Miami's Jake Scott (VII) and Dallas' Larry Brown (XXX).

VICTORY!
The youngest coach to win a Super Bowl, Jon Gruden had other reasons to celebrate, too. In his first year with his new team, he not only brought the Buccaneers to their first Super Bowl but also defeated the team that he had coached the previous four seasons.

EXTRA, EXTRA
It was big news when the Tampa Bay Buccaneers won Super Bowl XXXVII. The team never before had even appeared in the NFL's title game.

Index

NFL Creative
6245 Bristol Parkway, PMB 269
Culver City, California 90230

www.nfl.com

NFL Creative Staff: Editor-in-Chief: John Wiebusch. General Manager: Bill Barron. Executive Editor: Tom Barnidge. Managing Editor: John Fawaz. Project Art Director: Bill Madrid. Associate Art Directors: Susan Kaplan, Jackie O'Camb. Project Editors: Matt Marini, Joe Velazquez. Director-Photo Services: Paul Spinelli. Photo Editor: Kevin Terrell. Manager-Photo Services: Tina Resnick. Director-Manufacturing: Dick Falk. Director-Print Services: Tina Dahl. Manager-Computer Graphics: Sandra Gordon.